KINGDOM
Love

BILLIE I. REYNOLDS

Xulon PRESS

Kingdom Love
God's love is in action around the world
by Billie I. Reynolds

Printed in the United States of America.

ISBN 9781498455756

www.xulonpress.com

Contact Billie I. Reynolds at:

azreynolds@juno.com
kingdom-love.com
kingdom-love.com

DEDICATION

"I was glad when they said unto me, 'Let us go to the house of the Lord.'"   *Psalm 122:1 NKJV*

A friend invited me to attend their church youth group in 1941 when my young world seemed hopeless. Life has never been the same, thanks to the prayers and countless hours of friendship, fellowship, teaching and challenging from caring youth and the adult leaders. Pastor Clarence B. Holland, whose youth was spent working in the coal mines, encouraged all to come play volley ball and games for a couple of hours each Saturday night from the 1930's –1970's. Summers we attended Camp at Seven Springs, AZ., transported by one member's cleaned up cattle truck.

Our Capitol Methodist Youth Family, produced a nationally known commercial artist, a professor of Greek at Duke Seminary, four Elders in the Methodist Church, a Wycliffe Translator, several outstanding nurses and teachers, an opera singer, businessmen and women, salesmen, homemakers, bus drivers, counselors, entrepreneurs and veterans of WWII and the Korean War. They made life better where ever they lived and to my knowledge, none went to prison.

Those still living are extended family, spiritually enriched, imperfect human beings, who are blessed to be both givers and receivers of Kingdom Love. I pray young people worldwide should be so fortunate.

TABLE OF CONTENTS

INTRODUCTION

'The Kingdom of heaven is at hand.' Heal the sick, cleanse the lepers, raise the dead, cast out demons. Freely you have received, freely give."

Matt 10:8 NKJ V

GOD'S INCREDIBLE KINGDOM LOVE

*R*efresh your heart and mind. Break away from the bad news and read about the positive Kingdom Love impacting millions every day. Though non-believers scoff, this book presents measureable, genuine proof of God's blessings through Kingdom Love.

Kingdom love is the opposite of war, bloodshed, killing, and power hungry leaders. Amidst the human problems, God's spiritually led men and women implement Kingdom Love by healing the sick, feeding the hungry and inspiring hope in the neediest. God's wise economy never wastes or loses any good deed or drop of love. His simple message worldwide is "Love God and love your neighbor as yourself."

Kingdom Love demonstrates the attributes of the Father, Creator; Jesus, the Redeemer; and Holy Spirit, the Comforter in action. It moves through pain, oppression, the terror of war and eases the ache of grinding labor. In spite of bad news, its truth and joy heal broken hearts and bodies, bringing laughter and hope to young and old across the world. Kingdom Love respects all races, genders, and ages.

Kingdom Love soars across the glaciered peaks, arid deserts, rice paddies, congested cities, mud huts, displaced-person camps, and Ebola clinics in Africa. Billions practice simple acts of love with positive, measureable results that go unreported amidst the ugly and negative news. World agencies report extreme improvement in the quality of life for 80% of the world's population since 1950.

Harmony and happiness, not gunshots, hum in the air while diverse international and local groups deliver semi-trucks of food to refugee cities in the middle of deserts or where tsunamis and earthquakes wrench houses and lives apart. Love and science work together for human-kind. Kingdom-love-inspired doctors travel around the world without pay, sharing their knowledge and skills. It activates thousands of volunteers to pack tons of food and medical supplies for fellow human beings whose needs are great. Human concord springs from caring millions through churches and humanitarian organizations as they fulfill God's great commandments. As a result of Kingdom Love, new believers are coming into the faith at a rate of 125,000 per week.[1]

Kingdom love arises from compassionate people like the Samaritan who cared for a fallen stranger and like the people you meet in this book.

a) Bono of U2 Band fame, who for 30 years has raised funds and awareness so forgiveness of poor nations debt occurred and medicine is available to heal HIV/AIDS victims in Africa and the world.

b) The Albanian Muslims whom until recently no one knew about. They saved 2,000 Jews from Nazi extermination during WWII, protecting their 'Jewish brothers.'[2]

c) Chinese Christians have benefited from two Christian missionaries whom Mao kicked out of China. They built large humanitarian organizations serving the world as well as bolstering the Chinese Christians.

d) A tiny man in simple clothes utilized the principals of Christian love, truth and non-violence, for 30 years, leading India's people from British rule into a democracy, without firing a shot.

---

[1] World Christian Encyclopedia
[2] Besa" by Norman H. Gershman

e) A young multi-millionaire stopped working for himself in order to feed nine million people for over four years, then later in life founded the Boys' Clubs of America as well as UNICEF and CARE for the United Nations.

Five widows whose husbands were killed by the Auca Indians' spears learned the Auca language and took Auca New Testaments into that primitive world. The Aucas converted to Christianity, insured their land and Acua college graduates run their nation.[3]

Kingdom love stirs hearts of little grandmothers who share prayers, donate hand knitted sweaters, share some money which combines with millions to support the world's poor and oppressed.

Because men and women are God's hands and feet on earth, when led by the Holy spirit they change the world. These true chapters, full of action, adventure, hope and healing are just a drop in the ocean of Kingdom love.

---

[3] "Gates of Splendor" by Elisabeth Elliot

Umcor, The Passonate Heart Of The United Methodist Church

For the kingdom of God is not eating and drinking,
but righteousness and peace and joy in the Holy
Spirit. Therefore he who serves Christ in these things
is acceptable to God and approved by men. Therefore
let us then pursue the things which make for peace
and the things by which one may edify another."
                                   Rom 14: 17-19 NKJV

*A*frica sounded thrilling!
    "We are going to have an opening in Africa for a new radio station," said Dr. Harry J. Haines, General Secretary of UMCOR. " I wondered if you and your husband might like to talk to me about it and consider going there to run it?" asked a youngish, gray haired man following a TV show our group produced at the 1968 Portland, Oregon United Methodist Women's convention.

    Attending the Methodist church's, Television, Radio and Film Commission (TRAFCO) class, a group of pastors and me were learning to effectively place our public service radio, TV programs and films, as well as produce them. My husband and I operated our own advertising agency in Salem, following his six years with Eugene's KVAL-TV.

I called hubby, Bill, to see if he would drive up to meet Dr. Haines. But the idea of hot, untamed Africa held no appeal to him whatsoever! Dr. Haines quickly found a couple for that station who truly desired to serve in Africa.

Typical of Methodist history, Dr. Haines wanted to expand the Methodist Committee on Overseas Relief, (MCOR) its worldwide arm of kingdom love. From the beginning the brothers, John and Charles Wesley, led both social service and evangelistic activities.

John and Charles Wesley had visited colonial Georgia with James Oglethorpe, sadly returning to England in 1737, having failed at developing an effective church for settlers and natives. However, shortly after their return to England in 1738 both John and Charles' lives were forever changed in separate meetings two nights apart. They had spent their lives following all the Anglican Church's laws and doing good works, but did not really have personal heart relationships with Jesus. Charles a moderate drinker, experienced his spiritual revelation at a prayer meeting In his home as they prayed for his healing. He was never drawn to drink liquor after that. John attended the Moravians' Aldersgate Prayer Meeting, where during the reading of Luther's preface to the Book of Romans, "I felt my heart strangely warmed. I felt I did trust in Christ, Christ alone for salvation; and an assurance was given me that He had taken away my sins, even mine, and saved me from the law of sin and death."

When they shared their joy both Charles and John knew they had experienced what their dying father, Samuel, had asked them on his deathbed. "Do you have His assurance? Do you know and trust His grace?" They both had followed the church laws with study, prayer and founding the Holy Club at Oxford. They helped jailed prisoners and shared food with the hungry. However, after Aldersgate, they passionately shared the love of God with the world with zealous desire for the salvation of sinners, the nurture and edification of believers, and compassion for the powerless, oppressed and dispossessed.

History credits John and Charles Wesley with saving England from a destructive revolution like France endured. The Anglican Church would not permit the Wesley's to preach, nor their poor converts to partake of communion in the churches. The Wesley's laity preaching aided citizens' religious and moral lives, which the established church had been unable and even unwilling to bring about. They encouraged the human need and desire of salvation, revelation of God's grace in Christ, the need for spiritual transformation and experience of redemption through faith.

English society changed for the better. Organized weekly class meetings in all communities provided sharing and praying for each other, as well as learning how to read and write. As John traveled around the British Isles, he carefully went through the lists of each class, watching for the advancements in holiness. Did they experience peace, power, and joy then turn this love into mission service? Evangelists on Wesley's teams also had to be social reformers. John divided England into circuits, appointed preachers and organized men to work outside of England.

At the 1774 Christmas Conference in America, Thomas Coke and Francis Asbury formally birthed the Methodist church in the United States. These superintendents adopted the Articles of Religion and established a polity (form of church government). United Brethren Leader Philip Otterbein consecrated Asbury as Bishop. Ironically their two churches were reunited in 1969 as the United Methodist Church.

The Wesleys influenced another great organization reaching the world's lost and disenfranchised in the 1860's when a young William Booth learned preaching and social service under the Methodist church in London. In 1865, Booth founded The Salvation Army, one of the world's greatest sources of Kingdom love.

For 240 years the Methodists impacted the USA, moving west with the pioneers and implanting the nation with the Wesleyan "vision of holy love and vital piety."

Early American Methodism and the frontier population developed an instant liking for each other. Tireless circuit riders and missionaries preached the saving, hope-filled message to the fearful, lonely and displaced. With an annual allowance of $24, Circuit riders were as poor as their parishioners. Driven by intense activism, and ardent devotion to God they regularly saw miracles of physical healing, emotional depressions lifted and conversions to belief. They sought out the neglected, the destitute, those for whom no other cared. No man, woman or child was so ignorant, so miserable and forsaken and degraded as to be beneath their notice. There was a saying when the weather was bad, "There won't be nothin' outside today, except birds and the Methodist preacher."

Some preachers carried a bedroll and planned to stay for a few days, holding a Camp Meeting, which took the place of the weekly English Class meetings the Wesley's held. Homesteaders attended all-day or week-long revivals that drew families and neighbors into a loving community in the harsh wilderness. Methodists welcomed blacks, Indians and immigrants. However, regional prejudices in the north and south over slavery split them into a trio of churches; the Blacks, the South, and the North formed separate congregations until 1939 when they merged again.

Interestingly, the United Methodist Church's worldwide compassionate work of justice, mercy and humility came into motion by the founding of Methodist Committee Overseas Relief (MCOR) in 1940, now UMCOR with the United Brethren on board. UMCOR, begun under Bishop Herbert Welch, grew rapidly under the leadership of Dr. Harry Haines, a New Zealand pastor to China until Mao tossed him and his wife out along with all the foreign missionaries. Mao then killed millions of Chinese Christians who would not renounce their Lord.

From 1966 onward, Haines led the growth of this branch of Methodist service around the world to 62 countries and five continents. UMCOR began working with FEMA. They resettled thousands of Asian refugees, supporting many more within their nations. In its first 50 years, United Methodists donated more than $200,000,000 to UMCOR and relocated 50,000 refugees. More than 1,200 UM volunteers serve in Haiti, Jamaica, Mexico, other Caribbean countries and the USA.

Drought in Ethiopia, and other African nations attracted UMCOR services, along with the Mexico City earthquake in 1985. Bosnia and Herzegovina were aided by their Non-Governmental field offices developing assistance and long term projects in local communities. Liberia and Azerbaijan received UMCOR assistance as did the USA after the 9/11 terrorist bombing of New York City and the Pentagon. Following Hurricane Katrina, UMCOR was deeply involved with restoration and is still sending home- building teams to the Gulf Coast. They send money to fight AIDS in Africa; food and medical aid to the Philippines; and provide mosquito nets for Africa. If there is a disaster, a need for people to be helped and to hear the comforting words of God, UMCOR is there, demonstrating kingdom love.

An interesting side note regarding Dr. Haines concerns the fruit from New Zealand (NZ) that we call Kiwi. A young Harry Haines and a leader from the NZ Chamber of Commerce brought these Chinese Gooseberries to Harry and David's in Medford, Oregon. No one liked that name. Innovative Haines said, "New Zealanders are called Kiwis...let's call them Kiwi fruit." And thus the popular fruit was introduced to the USA and the world, just as under Dr. Haines creative leadership UMCOR's reach broadened around the world.

UMCOR continues under the able direction of successful leaders, like Denise Honeycutt, Deputy General Secretary and Thomas Kemper, General Secretary.

Each of the eight Board Member is responsible for specific international programs.

God inspired the loving hearts, minds and spirits of the Wesleys in the 1700s, spawning the United Methodist Church with its world-wide missions, which in turn inspired William Booth to found The Salvation Army. Both groups continue believing and practicing John Wesley's mission statement: "The world is my parish."

1) John Wesley's Journal
Dr. J Harry Haines: "Into Our Third Century" with introduction by Alan K. Waltz, Editor.
'Kiwi Name Story' from the Celebration of Life Service for Dr. J. Harry Haines.

WHAT KINGDOM LOVE DID, DOES AND IS DOING

THE SALVATION ARMY
"America's Favorite Charity"

"...for I was hungry and you gave Me food; I was thirsty and you gave Me something to drink; I was a stranger and you welcomed Me; I was naked and you gave Me clothing I was sick and you took care of Me; I was in prison and you came to Me."
Matthew 25:35-36 (NKJ)

Young children working 60-80 hour weeks in terrible conditions are a reality in parts of India and much of Asia today, just as it was during the early 1800's in London. One of those boys, William Booth, was apprenticed at age fourteen to a Pawn Broker to support his family after his father's death. He saw first hand the deplorable lives of the poor which drew him to study for the ministry at night. He had seen families become hungry and helpless when the breadwinner died or there was serious illness. If people knew that God still loves them and they repented from sin, he believed they could become the person God created them to be. He attended seminary until he found he was attracted to the Arminianism concepts preached by John and Charles Wesley and their ministry to folks in jail and debtors' prison. He felt God-led to the Methodist's belief in grace and mercy for all.

Friends introduced him in 1830 to Catherine Mumford to whom he was attracted from that first moment. A deep lifelong love developed as her feelings for William were mutual. William Booth was the visionary, enthusiastic preacher and she the calm, philosophical creative balance. Well ahead of the Feminist's NOW and ERA movements in 21st Century America, Catherine convinced William that God created men and women as equals. When she had thought and studied things thoroughly she would have 'settled views'. (Her mind would be made up and settled on the correct response).

The Booths were a very compassionate couple who felt with deep sorrow the wretchedness of London's poor. In Hackney, a London suburb, William served as a pastor under the leadership of the Methodists. William Booth wanted to help feed and make daily life better for the 'throw away' people to whom he preached. Under his fervent and genuine preaching great numbers of people became believers.

The Church of England seemed indifferent to the poor and did little to assist the ignorant multitudes huddling in shanties, resorting to stealing and other crime to survive. William and Catherine felt compelled by God to make these lost souls' lives better spiritually and materially, giving them hope. They believed that all human beings can become children of God. Many have not been exposed to the love of Jesus Christ, His death on the cross, and His desire to rescue them from sin.

To carry out his mission William parted from the Methodist church "without a friend or a farthing" and conducted revivals in the open air with dramatic, impassioned, colorful sermons that converted thousands of individuals. He sometimes came home with blood and bruises from the detractors' efforts; and 'sorrowed' that he had not reached the rowdies who jeered and threw stones.

London's vice-ridden East End was a cesspool of poverty-stricken, drink-sodden men, women and roughnecks. "Soap, soup and salvation" from Booth's ardent efforts helped the disreputable converts begin earning money honestly; sober up; and feed and take care of their families. The results were safer neighborhoods

and less crime. Local businessmen and philanthropists became suffi-
ciently impressed by these positive results that they agreed to finance
Booth's ministries through The London Christian Mission.

They paid Booth a modest base salary allowing him to concentrate on his work without concern about a roof over his head.

Christmas Day 1865, two births occurred; 1) The Salvation Army
and 2) Eva, was born, the seventh child of William and Catherine
Booth, who became one of its greatest leaders. Booth, bearded and
wearing a frock- coat, called the other six children and pulled back
the blanket from the basket so the older children could see their new
baby sister and quietly said, "Here is God's Christmas gift, your
sister Eva."

The Booth home had a large upstairs playroom where the children enthusiastically enjoyed life. Love, music and humor as well as
piety filled the house. Besides being a good mother to seven children,
Catherine worked with the unfortunate, visiting the sick, assisting the
elderly, and pleading with drunkards to stop drinking. Her famous
statement was, "Tell a man the truth about himself, then tell the truth
about God, tell the truth about his obligation." She believed that "A
few good people can effectively minister to much larger numbers."

William Booth launched his concept of a trained army of people
working for the conversion of all mankind 150 years ago, now known
worldwide as The Salvation Army (TSA). Booth envisioned this
army with its red, yellow and blue 'Blood and Fire' flag spreading
the Gospel, waging a relentless war on sin and battling social evils in
every corner of the world. Their vision has not changed, just adapted
to contemporary times and needs.

Realizing music spoke to people's hearts; Booth began the street
corner preaching with band music and gospel songs. Monies earned
by the band concerts, meetings and gifts from donors went directly
to feed and cloth the poor. By 1883, there were 400 TSA brass bands.

Booth bought Congress Hall, a large old building in London's
East End, which could seat 6,000, to serve as a meeting place for the
growing crowds as well as a warehouse for food to share with the
hungry. Eventually The Salvation Army (TSA) surrounded London
with TSA meeting halls like the Grecian Theater and Regent Hall,
an old skating rink.

Jeers and frequently hurled rotten fruit and vegetables splattered uniforms and faces of band members. Businessmen started stationing guards around the meetings to control mob misbehavior. Catherine likened these events to fighting a war. "Fighting in ministry has to do with exerting great energy in God's behalf in spite of opposition or great trial." When confronted by Social Darwinism's dislike of The Salvation Army's help for the vulnerable and disabled, Booth responded, "They believe in the survival of the fit; the TSA believes in the salvation of the unfit."

Long before Eliza Doolittle in the musical "My Fair Lady," Eva Booth was working with the poorest of the flower girls in London. She sold flowers, giving the money to the "Army" and the poorest of the girls. Some of the bosses disliked her inviting the other girls to TSA meetings and preaching to them. That didn't stop Eva's work with prostitutes and children. Eva was fearless. Throughout her lifetime she faced many intimidating situations head on, turning them into win-win situations. She negotiated successfully for God's work with the poor and rich, the weak and powerful. When he ran out of solutions, General Booth would tell his oldest son and confidant, Bramwell, "Send Eva; she can handle this."

Undaunted by taunts and harassment, adults and young people who came to know the Lord and believe in The Salvation Army cause, eagerly begged to join the TSA as new cadets. To train and educate this new army, Booth envisioned an academy which soon became a reality, The International Training College at Clapton. Today generations of Army families still study, train, sign the Soldier's Covenant, and then march out into the world waging war on sin, powered by God's redeeming love. Their prayers are known as "kneel drills", their tithes are "firing cartridges", and their buildings are "citadels" for the growing army of soldiers and cadets.

Not everyone liked the marching bands of "Lassies and Lads" in their blue uniforms designed and sewn by Catherine. Some towns tried to outlaw the 'marching music' as they headed to meetings. Indifferent leaders permitted hooligans to rough up band members, often putting TSA band members in jail. Thanks to Eva, Parliament passed an act that permitted TSA bands to play on the streets and march to the meetings.

The Salvation Army pioneered immense humanitarian programs like those currently being carried on by hundreds of non-governmental organizations. In war and peace, good times and natural disasters, and in the most hideous and ugly places with the most desperate in any nation where the gospel is permitted, The Salvation Army is there; nurturing peoples' souls and lives with tender love so that they can become who God naturally intended them to be.

Like wisdom, love is vindicated by her deeds. No one can explain this remarkable force. Rather than weakness weeding out the less than perfect through natural selection, love reinforces and renews, turning lives around.

The TSA is known for feeding the world's hungry, drilling clean water wells, teaching people to plant and store crops, educating children, treating the ill, building hospitals and bringing love and hope to all.

Little wonder that The Salvation Army quickly spread throughout England, across the channel to France and the rest of Europe. It's estimated that Booth preached over 60,000 sermons before his final words: "The promises of God are sure, if you only believe." By the time Booth died in 1912, The Salvation Army was established in 58 countries. Today you will find them in over 126 nations alongside the most helpless and hopeless. Emboldened by the Holy Spirit, The Salvation Army men and women carry out the dreams and visions Jesus gave to William Booth, reaching out to every person on the face of the earth with the story of God's redemption and love.

---

1) *New King James Bible*
2) *The official name of this organization is: 'The Salvation Army'.*
3) *"Christianity in Action" The History of the International Salvation Army by Henry Gariepy 2009*
4) *The Salvation Army's Soldier's Covenant*

Soldier's Covenant

" *Having accepted Jesus Christ as my Saviour and Lord, and desiring to fulfill my membership of His church on earth as a soldier of The Salvation Army, I now, by God's grace enter into a sacred covenant.*

I believe and will live by the truths of the word of God expressed in the Salvation Army's eleven articles of faith:

We believe that the Scriptures of the Old and New Testaments were given by inspiration of God; and that they only constitute the Divine rule of Christian faith and practice.

We believe that there is only one God, who is infinitely perfect, the Creator, Preserver, and Governor of all things, and who is the only proper object of religious worship.

We believe that there are three persons in the Godhead – the Father, the Son and the Holy Ghost – undivided in essence and co-equal in power and glory. We believe that in the person of Jesus Christ the Divine and human natures are united, so that He is truly and properly God and truly and properly man.

We believe that our first parents were created in a state of innocence, but by their disobedience they lost their purity and happiness; and that in consequence of their fall all men have become sinners, totally depraved and as such are justly exposed to the wrath of God.

We believe that the Lord Jesus Christ has, by His suffering and death, made atonement for the whole world so that whosoever will may be saved.

We believe that repentance towards God, faith in our Lord Jesus Christ and regeneration by the Holy Spirit is necessary to salvation.

We believe that we are justified by grace, through faith in our Lord Jesus Christ; and that he that believeth hath the witness in himself.

We believe that continuance in a state of salvation depends upon continued obedient faith in Christ.

We believe that it is the privilege of all believers to be wholly sanctified, and that their whole spirit and soul and body may be preserved blameless unto the coming of our Lord Jesus Christ.

We believe in the immortality of the soul; in the resurrection of the body; in the general judgment at the end of the world; in the eternal happiness of the righteous; and in the endless punishment of the wicked."

In addition they promise to be responsive to the Holy Spirit's leading; growing in grace through worship, Bible reading, prayer... uphold Christian integrity, not allowing unclean, unworthy, untrue, profane dishonest immoral thoughts; to maintain Christian ideas in all relationships and uphold the sanctity of marriage and family life as well as be a faithful steward of time, gifts, and possessions, body, mind and spirit. They agree to abstain from alcoholic drink, tobacco, and non-medical use of addictive drugs, gambling pornography, and the occult. They promise to be faithful to the purposes for which God raised up the Salvation Army, sharing the good news of Jesus Christ, endeavoring to win others to Him and in His name caring for the needy and disadvantaged.

A DYNAMO OF KINGDOM LOVE AND POWER

It is good to give thanks to the Lord, to sing praises to your name, O Most High; to declare your stead-fast love in the morning, and your faithfulness by night, to the music of the lute, the harp, to the melody of the lyre. For you O Lord, have made me glad by your work; at the works of your hands I sing for joy.
Psalm 92:1-4 (NRSV)

*A*n auburn haired child of seven known as Eva, marched out onto the stage of London's Memorial hall. Filled to capacity, the crowd had been singing lustily with The Salvation Army Band until in a clear voice, she sang one of the favorite hymns of the day. Instantly a hush came over the crowd until she invited them to join in the chorus. Evangeline Booth, now known as Eva began her impact on the world's religious ministry for the next seventy-five years.

Gifted with musical talents, a lovely speaking voice and poise, fearless Eva possessed the rare ability to negotiate with enemies so that it was 'win' for them as well as The Salvation Army. In addition to an uncanny creativity in staging and musical arts, she developed great business acumen, rare for a circa 1870's London woman.

Eva sold flowers, dressed in tattered clothes, working with the roughest and toughest rogues on London streets. When she was not solving difficult social problems, she played the concertina, guitar, harp, and piano; wrote poetry and music. Her growing fame and success around London as she reached into tough neighborhoods warranted an invitation to Parliament whose members wanted to learn about her preaching.

From the House of Lords, Quaker Statesmen John Bright, Earl Cairns, Disraeli's Lord Chancellor and The Earl of Shaftsbury invited her to parliament to hear her preach.

"Talk to us like you are on the pavement. Look on me as a drunkard," said Shaftsbury.

Eva began, "I should tell you that you are a fine fellow and I should want to know why you treated yourself like that, spoiling your looks and making yourself ridiculous. I should say to you, you are worth more than that and it is time you should know it."

Cairns played the part. "I can't help it!"

"I should ask you to kneel with us and ask God's help."

"But I'm not quite convinced."

"Then I should remind you of Christ on the Cross. He did that to save. He did not die for nothing."

"That's what you mean by the Gospel?" asked Cairns.

She added, "Yes, this is what we mean by the Gospel."

The statesmen took TSA Captain Eva Booth, to tea with strawberries and cream.

She made them aware of the year-long battle in the city of Torquay where some folks disliked The Salvation Army bands playing music while marching to their meeting halls. Thanks to Eva, Parliament passed an Act of Permitting 400 TSA Bands to play anywhere in England.

General Booth sent Eva to the infamous ghetto of Marylebone. She worked with the poorest of the poor and gangs. She would find a gang leader, help him get a job, donate to his food needs; and soon his whole gang was on her side. When General Booth said she was needed elsewhere, the police requested in writing that she stay; her work was making such a difference in conditions of the people, as well as reducing crime. Young and old were traveling long distances to hear her exhortations, many becoming reconciled to God's love.

Her sincerity and genuineness seem to overcome the rawest hearts. She knew what she was doing and felt the sermon was "the gun shot" to shatter the defenses that souls had erected against God. She didn't want sermons to be filled with coarse language and would say "do not tread on velvet carpets with hobnail boots – let your touch be gentle, tender as the wounds to be healed. Never allow yourself the thought that common people are common to God; all men and women, even lost ones, were made in the Divine Image ... bring forth the best robes and put on him or her."

Many Salvation Army student cadets came from the streets following their conversions. Some who joined the ranks of the Army were untutored robbers, drunkards and gamblers. At age twenty-two, Evangeline was made head of the International Training College at Clapton. General Booth believed this converted rag-tag Army, with the aid of the Holy Spirit, could and would win the world for God.

Once converted cadets were taught to read and write, they learned how to: 1) bring new believers to kneel at the Penitent Form; 2) teach converts to become real Christians; 3) help converts deepen their Spiritual life; 4) instruct converts in their heritage as reborn followers of Jesus Christ; and 5) value their morning Holiness Meetings.

Clean uniforms, clean fingernails, were important, but the basis was not what you do, "but how much you love, for love is the fulfillment of God's law."

Her sweet and humble personality was backed by a rod of steel character. Training was rigid as well as practical. No one would dream of talking back to the 150 lb redheaded, lady standing 5'10" who held no fear of anything or anyone. "Nothing that did not serve the Kingdom was included in the full curriculum."

Like any program that brings social changes, The Salvation Army (TSA) faced conflicts. Sometimes members were roughed up, jailed and fined. Salvationists from other cities would come to their rescue. The contrasting views of 'believers in dynamic evangelism' VS the 'static persons in church pew' has been with us since Jesus Christ walked the earth. Christians still struggle over the most effective ways to share the Gospel, but General Booth and his army knew their calling was 'hands on out in the world.'

Eva followed the orders given by her father, as she believed his mind was divinely guided. The Salvation Army had reached France and most of Europe when in 1880, 1882 and 1886 Salvationists set forth to Canada and the United States.

It is reported that when The Salvation Army first arrived in NYC they knocked on the doors of businesses; One German woman who kept a saloon, cried out, "Salvationists! My God, Hans, lock the doors."

Thirty year old Evangeline arrived in Toronto, Canada, and moved into a haunted house as the price was right. Her doctor had recommended a change of residence to allow healing of some health problems. In Canada she was riding horses and slept when possible in a tent in her back yard. She was once again working long days teaching and preaching to the Indians as well as the city dwellers. The Salvation Army founded hospitals for women and children in Newfoundland, and sent aid to the Armenian people when they suffered from a massacre in 1896. Leader, Evangeline, now known by her full name, didn't do things alone, but was the spiritual and creative leader of a full staff of TSA worker units. There were no reports regarding ghosts in the haunted house, or she may have converted them to be Salvationists.

Brother Bramwell became the second General of TSA upon William Booth's death. And to his consternation Evangeline set out with a team of eight for the Klondike gold rush where…"a wild stampede of over-eager prospectors were releasing the pent-up avarice of mankind." These eight Salvationists made it to Dawson City, rowing nearly five hundred miles in boats; their hands blistered, and then carried loads on their backs. The Salvationists had fine audiences with miners who poured gold dust into the collection plate. They built their quarters on donated land. A backslider (former Christian) became their first convert. Upon his reconciliation, he enrolled as a soldier of TSA having gambled and drunk away his $7,000 gold strike.

Moving on to Skagway, Alaska, Evangeline and the Salvationists hiked up snowy Chilcoot Pass with their supplies and canoe, along with the gold seekers. Reaching the summit and rowing across the Barnett Lake, they managed to cook Thanksgiving dinner for 300 men who had been working their icy gold claims.

Back at Skagway, the homesick miners, struggling in the harsh climate and dog-eat-dog environment, flocked to the TSA where familiar music, warm coffee and cocoa were served in the afternoons.

Skagway was ruled by Soapy Smith who owned the bar and brothel, as well as the telegraph service where people sent massages home when they hit a strike. However, the wire service was a fraud. The supposed electrical cord running into the water was just a wire with no connection. A miner hitting it big would wire his family he had a strike and was on his way home. Soon he was feted with free drinks at Soapy's saloon. Later his body would be found after Soapy's goons stole his gold. Upset that more and more miners attended the Salvationists' homespun music and warm friendship instead of coming to his bar to spend their money, Soapy Smith came to the Salvation camp with five of his armed body guards.

"Leave him to me," Evangeline told the others. She had seen him listening to her talks from time to time. She pulled Soapy aside into the wooded area.

"Why don't you give up this kind of life?" she asked

He told her that if he surrendered to the authorities it would mean his death. She spoke to him of a salvation that means victory over death. Amid the shadows of the forest they prayer together before Soapy Smith departed.

The next morning on the boat dock, Frank Reid pulled the fake telegraph cable out of the water for all to see. Soapy Smith shot Frank who fired back. Frank died immediately. Soapy lasted a couple of days, but denied the community the pleasure of putting him in the hanging noose.

In prior years other Salvationists had brought the gospel to the Tlinget Indians in their villages. Evangeline and her staff visited and found no fewer than 300 believers along the seaboard, many of whom spoke English. The natives pleaded that a TSA officer to be sent to lead them so they too could live life under The Salvation Army Flag. Her team met with the Indians; taught them; heard them sing and could see no reason to hold back any longer making them Salvation Army Soldiers. The Tlinget tribe is currently 85% Christian .

When called to America, Evangeline didn't realize she would serve the most prominent portion of her action-packed career from

1904-1934 as USA Commander. She was an immediate success in their largest and richest region. Like her father who had met with President McKinley, spoken to the Senate and spent time with Theodore Roosevelt, who called Booth "A steam engine in trousers," Evangeline attracted the powerful. She counted among her friends Presidents Herbert Hoover and Woodrow Wilson. She gave the prayer at the Democratic convention that elected F.D. Roosevelt.

During WWI Eva trained and sent to France, Salvation Directors and teams of "Lassies" where they made cocoa and doughnuts for the soldiers. The carefully selected lassies lived near the front lines, moving their tents as the battle lines changed.

"They were sent forth to love the souls of men as God loved them. Unless self be forgotten their work would be in vain." Under dire conditions these lassies under the guidance of their leaders, daily made 225 gallons of cocoa, 2500 doughnuts, 50 pies, 800 pancakes, as well as fried eggs. The girls prayed with scared young soldiers before battle and the wounded in the hospitals. At the war's end Cardinal James Gibbons of NYC headed a fund raiser for The Salvation Army that raised $15,000,000. (Their goal was $12,000,000). Pres. Wilson awarded Evangeline the Distinguished Service Medal. She was honored by British Prime Minister Lloyd George; General John J. Pershing, head of American Forces WWI; and France's Marshal Foch and President Clemenceau.

Evangeline Booth was sought after by the great leaders of the world. Often she stood in halls filled with thousands and was so sincere that her audience would be in profound silence for minutes. People worldwide wanted to hear Evangeline, who disliked traveling, but like her father, journeyed globally to bolster TSA. She started at the Army's bottom level as a Cadet worked up to Sergeant by age fifteen and earned her way up through the ranks until her 1934 appointment as TSA General. It meant leaving the USA and returning to The Salvation Army Headquarters, in her native England.

She was given a New York City ticker tape parade to say thank you for the WWI efforts and her overall services. Her superstar farewell from America was held at a packed Madison Square Garden; hundreds stood outside. Her greatest happiness was not traveling and speaking to thousands, or meeting the leaders of the great nations, but in the salvation of persons from despair and hopelessness into wholeness through God's redeeming love. Her files were filled with letters from people saved from a life of sin; free to find their Creator's purpose for them. When her role as General ended, Evangeline returned to Hartsdale, NY where she died at age 85.

The full impact of The Salvation Army's one hundred fifty year history would not be complete without Evangeline's 85-year life and dedication to the service of others. She made The Salvation Army goals her life goals, even when it meant turning down a loving proposal of marriage and prestigious offers in the business world. The entire Booth progeny gave their lives to The Salvation Army cause. All married and had families, except Evangeline. Her life touched thousands around the world from every walk of life. She reached out with a Godly spirit that enabled her to be the instrument of miraculous healings and problem solving across the world. Like Evangeline, The Salvation Army doesn't flinch at toughs or squalor. No one is unworthy because Christ's death on the Cross offers salvation to each person. All people deserve to hear God's message of hope, the reason The Lord's Salvation Army still marches, fighting sin and bringing kingdom love to the world.

"General Evangeline Booth of the Salvation Army" P.W. Wilson (C Scribner's 1948

DRUNK TO DRY: KINGDOM LOVE'S POWER TO CHANGE

"The Lord is not slack concerning His promise, as some count slackness, but is longsuffering toward us, not willing that any should perish but that all come to repentance.   *2 Peter 3:9 NKJV*

"The Bowery, the Bowery…I'll never go there anymore." – These are lines from an old New York City song from the turn of the century. It refers to the roughest, toughest part of NYC, the home of the boozers. In 1908 "the Bowery (Peter Stuyvesant called it his bouwerie) was home to poets gone mad with dipsomania, hollow-eyed and chalky-faced dope addicts who once had been men of affairs, bedraggled old women who shrilly screamed their imprecations on passersby, young girls who would huckster their very souls for a drink… all famished ghosts whose real selves had snatched at life and missed."

The central hangouts for drunks, like "The Doctor's," were cesspools where beer was served with two straws and a nickel whiskey shot. They had flop rooms, commonly known as "dead-houses," or the bums' headquarters. As many as fifty men, after pan- handling all day for coins for booze, would occupy a room. If the bum was drunk enough he could sleep with the vermin and stench until 5:00 A.M., then must leave so the place could be cleaned for the day's business.

One of the Bowery regulars for a three-year period was Henry Milans, a former editor for all the major New York City papers, but had permitted alcohol to take control of his life. From the peak of success he surrendered it all to booze, not caring about anyone or anything as long as there was some alcohol. When former friends attempted to help him by giving him money he would buy more booze. When they gave him nice clothes he would sell them at the shops and buy used clothes and pocket the difference for booze.

Once while he was sleeping on a park bench, someone stole his clothes, leaving him with underwear and no shoes. He walked barefoot from the Battery to the Bowery. He craved hot food and as he was about to step inside the Iron Gate to the soup kitchen, the gate slammed shut in his face. Henry wondered bitterly if heaven would be like that, all full, no more room, bums must stay out in the cold. In rare, sober moments his remorse tore at him and how low he had fallen. He sadly remembered his loving, praying mother who had faith in his dreams, and his broken-hearted wife, who walked away after years of Henry's losing battle with the bottle.

One day he got cash enough to drink himself into oblivion ending up in Bellevue Hospital where the doctor pointed out to a class of interns, "this patient has gone too far as his appetite is the biggest thing in his life, where his powers of resistance are broken down, where his body subsists almost entirely on alcohol, He is then positively incurable. Look at this man! He can never be cured!" They forgot to tell The Salvation Army that drunks are incurable.

The Salvation Army's 1908 innovation was called The Boozers Convention. A whole regiment of Salvationists ventured out at one time into the highways and byways of NYC, literally rounding up all the bums, drunkards, ne-er do-wells and broken pieces of humanity who could be found. Signs for Memorial Hall around NYC advertised "FREE EATS ALL DAY".

Churches and newspapers were extremely critical and skeptical. General Booth was concerned when word reached England as The Boozers Conventions were causing more comment than any Salvation Army effort since his own 'Darkest England Scheme.' "The movement in America is carrying out your command to followers: Go for souls, and go for the worst", the New York staff responded.

The inebriates were directed, led or carried to The Salvation Army Memorial Hall for the purpose of being invited, coaxed or jarred out of their self-loathing and hopelessness.

Inside Memorial Hall the putrid odor from the bums in the building contrasted with the music, hot food, music and speeches. Interspersed between talks were hymns like: "Where Is My Wandering Boy Tonight?"; "Nearer My God to Thee"; and "Rock of Ages."

Hungry alcoholics feasted on hot meals and coffee, listened to brief sermons and testimonies by ex-boozers. Scores of penitents made their way forward when alter calls were made. Male converts were taken to Men's Hotels and Industrial Homes operated by the Army where they could get on their feet. Women were sent to the Women's Hotel for care and treatment.

Though he managed to escape these events in the past, in 1910 Henry Milans attended the Boozers' Convention. He felt that they were praying directly at him. He was drawn to the altar with Envoy Katie Roberts. He still could not believe that he could be forgiven. They said "Good-night and God bless you" and invited him back to the weekly meetings. After attending several Boozers meetings, it penetrated his heart that God could make him sober. Touched by the Holy Spirit, Milans surrendered and wept for the first time in many years.

From that moment Henry never desired to drink again. Shortly after, he was back in the printing business. He wrote his mother that he was sober and in 'God's grace,' his letter arriving just days before she died. After he proved himself stable, his wife came back to him. Henry Milans once again was a happy and productive man and a frequent speaker at The Salvation Army Boozer meetings and conventions. Mentoring men became Henry's avocation through sobering them up and bringing them back into wholeness of life.

How does one measure the impact of renewed lives? At the February 12, 1914, "Ex Boozers Banquet" for reformed NYC drunks, The Salvation Army tabulated these statistics based on a combined total of 176 attendees:

> 3,238 years had been spent as drunkards, an average of 18 years per person;
>
> $1,291,500 was spent for their booze;

$645,750 was the amount of lost wages; and
$2,000,000 was the national loss in earning power.

Not measurable were the broken hearts and spirits of the families and loved ones.

NYC is but one city in the world where the patient and loving Salvationists offered then and now, grace and food while putting arms around smelly, difficult people. This Kingdom love demonstrates that God can and still does love them, no matter how far they have fallen, or how rotten their lives have become. God will forgive them.

However, the consequences of their drinking or drugs won't change:

People, whom they robbed, lied to, and cheated, may never trust them or want anything to do with them. Their neglected and abused or abandoned children may or may not ever want to see or hear from them. The hurt has been too great.

The penitent's wish to rekindle lost loves may remain futile.

Yet, The Salvation Army encourages persons restored from addictions, be it booze, drugs, gambling et al, to restore wholeness for the losses they created and to reach out to other addicts. Addicts will pay attention to persons who are former drunks and addicts, who with God's help, have whipped the problem.

According to science, per the Doctor at Bellevue Hospital, Henry Milans could not be healed; his alcoholism was too extreme. However, Milans was completely healed, not by medicine, but by God's Kingdom love, like millions around the world have been healed by that same power since time began.

Some of you might remember the infamous, hellish penal colony called Devil's Island. The Salvation Army persuaded the French Government in 1938 to permit them to work at rehabilitating the prisoners. They were able to repatriate 2,000 prisoners to acceptable lives out of 2,386; the balance were given merciful care.

Today, every nation where The Salvation Army operates recites similar stories as generations of troubled human beings are pulled from the oceans of sin into safe, productive lives once more. In any major city in 105+ nations, any who are hungry, addicted, suffering and in need, may enjoy TSA food, and a roof over their head. The men and women of The Salvation Army serve with loving hands and hearts. When thanked, they humbly ascribe all praise and credit for repatriation and salvation to God, Jesus Christ and the Holy Spirit.

2 Peter 3: 9 NKJV
All direct quotes from "Out of the Depths" by Clarence W. Hall
1935 Colonial Press, Inc., Clinton, Mass

THE SALVATION ARMY 2015

*"The Lord is a refuge for the oppressed, a stronghold
in times of trouble. Those who know your name will
trust in you, for you, Lord have never forsaken those
who seek you."*   *Psalm 9:9-10 NIV*

*W*hen the planes hit the New York City twin towers on 9/11,
The Salvation Army (TSA) was on the job immediately
and thereafter offering food and comfort to the responders. TSA was
in the Pacific for the Tsunami; in New Orleans when Katrina hit and
still is; ditto for 2010 earthquake in Haiti. When disasters strike TSA
is one of the primary 'boots on the ground' organizations.

If William and Catherine Booth have a bird's eye view from
Heaven, they can be pleased that The Salvation Army remains true to
its purpose and goals, while dealing with a changing world's realities.

The Lads and Lassies no longer wear the uniforms and bonnets,
but wear dark trousers or skirts with white shirts or blouses. Members
wear jackets and sweaters with TSA logo. Currently they operate in
126 nations, and continue to publish the War Cry magazine begun in
the 1890's.as well as other publications in 175 languages.

As of 2013 there were 14,966 Corps, outposts, societies, new
plants and recovery churches, including Goodwill Centers, managed by 5,117,923 officers, soldiers, employees, musicians, junior
and senior clients. They operate hostels, emergency lodges, and day-
care; serve the armed forces, assist individual communities, and provide health programs and education. "They are an unusual church

– Evangelical and Wesleyan. They don't practice the ordinances of Baptism and Communion. Music remains a vital part of the ministry with 2,000 bands worldwide. They remain pro-life and pro-traditional marriage."

It is interesting to note that there are high numbers of TSA officers and workers in Africa and many under-developed nations where they have had representation since 1883. Their largest African territory is Kenya with 350,000 soldiers.

Disaster Training is conducted in nations like Sri Lanka, India, Iraq, the UK and USA. One of their largest operations was New Orleans when Katrina hit.

They have build 500 new houses in Sri Lanka and 750 in Indonesia since the 2005 tsunami; they have built both temporary and permanent housing following the earthquake in Pakistan. They are training people around the globe in Kinshasas (Congo), Zimbabwe, Uganda, Rwanda, Nigeria, Romania, Chile, Brazil, Bolivia, Peru, India, The Philippines, Malawi, Tanzania and Kenya. However, due to hostile communism they are not in North Korea and struggle with Governmental harassment in Myanmar (Burma).

TSA obeys the laws and agreements of each nation where they serve; keeping current licenses in Russia and the separate nation of Ukraine.

TSA has developed unique water storage and transportation schemes to make water available in drought areas. The modern TSA does practical things like training 1000 Iraqis from humanitarian organizations across southern Iraq. These trained Iraqis are building schools and homes; water supplies; distributing livestock; and developing new jobs. This newly created Non-Government Organization (NGO) will be mentored by the TSA as these Iraqis continue to work for the recovery of the Iraqi people. Perhaps their motto in Ireland says what they do as well as anything…"Belief in Action"

The newest programs are a far cry from the TSA in 1968 when an exciting idea was developed for them to expand the Waioli Tea Room in the Manoa Valley, Honolulu. Founded in the 1890's The Tea Room provided jobs for the girls left 'in a family way' (pregnant) by visiting sailors. The Tea Room features wonderful full scale meals, but they are famous for special breads from very old recipes and fruit punch.

Tour buses making their way to the top of Mt. Tantalus stop to see the Robert Louis Stevenson (RLS) 'writing hut' given to TSA from the Claghorn Estate, formerly located where the Princess Kiaulani Hotel now stands. (Scotsman Claghorn was the father of Princess Kiaulani who was schooled in Scotland as preparation to become Queen of Hawaii). Positioned in the garden area, the RLS' hut contains mementoes of the famous author who frequently visited his fellow Scotsman and the Hawaiian King and Queen Liliuokalani. The Salvation Army was selected to own this hut as Stevenson strongly believed that 'self sacrifice for others is the Christ-like thing.' Also housed on the Waioli property are cottages where tired Salvation Army employees may come for rest and recuperation.

A former manager of the Tea Room thought that some dioramic scenes of Stevenson's books and a tramway up to the top of Mt. Tantalus would draw more people and bring added revenue. An artist-builder came over from the mainland and spent a few weeks researching the land above the Tea Room and how this could be accomplished. When drawings and cost estimates were given to appropriate Salvation Army leaders, they felt the concept was "far too exotic" for the Army's conservative image.

That has changed. TSA founded "Fight Against Sexual Abuse" to prevent child prostitution; provide rehabilitation and psychological care; and pleadings for helpless victims. Through these means TSA is rescuing hundreds of children and young adults from hell on earth.

Because TSA believes 'that poverty experienced by much of the world is unacceptable', it founded International Projects and Development Services (IPDS). Community development means transformation of communities by bringing the face of caring, hope and reconciliation along with basic human resources of food, water, health care and job development to the most destitute areas in the world.

TSA Major Barbara Blix, now in the Western Division USA, was among the first 9/11 responders to NYC ground zero. After six weeks protective coverings were made available to the workers. But like hundreds Major Barbara has severe health problems from breathing 'bad' air. She is currently being monitored, along with early 'ground zero' workers. This Major, a fifth generation member of the Army, like the Booths, accepts her compromised health, the price of serving The Lord in The Salvation Army. She retired in 2013.

TSA accepts your donations and prayers all year long. Shop their Good Will Industry stores offering well-priced goods and furnishings, operated by rehabilitated men and women. Remember these brief glimpses of TSA'S outreach as you share funds with those red kettle bell ringers at Christmas. Besides the tinkle of the bells or music from the bands, can you hear the music of love by The Salvation Army soldiers offering helping hands to our neediest brothers and sisters? Listen! Can you hear the sighs of joy from restored alcoholics, single moms and those rescued from sex trafficking?

Their current International Mission Statement says:

"The Salvation Army, an international movement, is an evangelical part of the universal Christian Church. Its message is based on the Bible. Its ministry is motivated by love for God. Its mission is to preach the gospel of Jesus Christ and meet human needs in His name without discrimination."

To Contact The Salvation Army:
E-mail: websa@salvationarmy.org or
http://www.salvationarmyusa.org
You will be asked to place your city, zip code, nation, and it will open to that area with the phone, address and information.
Phone: 1-800 725-2769

THE SALVATION ARMY TERMINOLOGY EXPLANATIONS

Salvationist	Active participant in The Salvation Army, employee or volunteer
Penitent Form	Altar where persons can pray, small or large
Penitents	Persons who seek repentance and prayer
The Salvation Army	The is part of the title TSA, not just Salvation Army
Imprecations	Evil Curses
Dipsomania	Insatiable craving for alcohol

Envoy	TSA trained leader and counselor, agent
Repatriate	Restore person to their home country; to wholeness
War Cry	Official Magazine of The Salvation Army
Dioramas	Three dimensional miniature scenes with models and lights
Good Will Industries	Wholesale and Retail stores and work outlets for TSA; Thrift Stores, Goodwill Drop Offs, Retail Stores; Gets People back on their feet and gainfully employed.
Concertina	Small accordion

BESA, MUSLIM
BROTHERLY LOVE

*J*ews in Albania, as elsewhere during WWII, were targeted for destruction by the conquering Germans. But their fate was altered by an ancient and sacrosanct Muslim Albanian principle known as Besa; one's word of honor. More than 2,000 Jews in Albania were spared the furnaces of Auschwitz, for they were hidden or otherwise sheltered by the Muslim population. Recognized in Israel as heroes, these brave people were not able to tell their story to the world until recently. They practiced **Besa,** to give sacrificial care for those in need, as their God taught them to live,

Norman H. Gershman has written a book entitled "Besa" which features the words of these brave people and their families along with photographs. He is a fine arts photographer whose work is represented in museums throughout the world. He spent five years traveling and interviewing the people who practiced Besa to save Jews. He reveals for the first time, a hidden period of history slowly emerging after the fall of Communism. Ordinary Albanian Muslims saved over 2,000 Jews, acting within their Albanian Muslim faith.

In Albania, when a person gives you his Besa to act in a certain way, he is committed to abide by it whatever the circumstances may require. This was coupled with another inherently Albanian folk principle – that of giving refuge to someone in need of help. Deeply rooted in Albanian culture and incorporated in the faith of Albanian Muslims, Besa is a code of honor. It dictates a moral behavior so absolute that non-adherence brings shame and dishonor on oneself and one's family. Simply stated, it demands that one take responsibility for the lives of others in their time of need.

Albania's Jews' tale of the rescue, just recently surfaced. Unfortunately their story remained unknown for many years because of the rigid, decades' long Communist regime in that country, which forbade any contact with outsiders.

This Islamic behavior of compassion and mercy celebrates the sanctity of life and a view of the other, the stranger, as indeed one's own close family member. Survivors relate that the Albanians vied with each other for the honor of sheltering fleeing Jews, a phenomenon unheard of in other European countries under the heel of the Nazis.

Here are a few of the comments by these compassionate and caring Muslims.

Lime Balla: "All of us villagers were Muslims. We were sheltering God's children under our Besa."[4]

Baba Haxhi Dede Reshat Bardbi: "We Bektashi see God everywhere, in everyone. God is in every pore and every cell, therefore all are God's children. There cannot be infidels. There cannot be discrimination. If one sees a good face one is seeing the face of God. God is Beauty. Beauty is God. There is no God but God."

Elida Bicaku: "My father and grandfather helped rescue twenty-six terrified Jews in a large barn and later in the forest, later taking them to the border for Yugoslavia. Both men are devout Muslims; neither would hurt a fly. My father is a secular Muslim. He says, 'Only trust in God, not even in the imam."

Nadire Proseku: " Why did we do it? We saw the Jews as brothers. As religious but liberal Muslims, we were only doing our duty. Now my grandson is an evangelical Christian. This is fine with my son and me. There is only one God."

The Domi Family: "Our parents were devout Muslims. They never saw a division among Muslims, Christians and Jews."

---

[4] All quotations are from the book "Besa" by Norman H. Gershman

Kujtim Civeja: "We are a traditional Muslim family of scholars in Berat for six generations. I have been a teacher and imam for thirty years. Our whole family both studies and practices our religion. The chemistry of life and good will lives in the Holy Koran…Our generation has a special feeling for the Jewish people. Our father wrote that when he had the opportunity and privilege to shelter so many Jewish families it gave him joy to put into practice his Islamic faith. To be generous is a virtue."

Higmete Zyma: "Why hide a Jew? We just did it. It was the thing to do. After all, our Jewish guest was a friend of our friends. Yes, we are Muslims, but secular Muslims."

Mehmet Ysref Frasberi: "All through the Nazi years we were never afraid to save lives. After the war the communists arrested and imprisoned my father. He was guilty of being an intellectual. We lived with the Koran's teaching to take care of the other."

Ismet Shpuza: "It seems strange to be asked why my father did what he did for this Jewish family. Besa is a tradition of the entire nation of Albania."

Hamdi Mece: "All life is precious and given by God. To save a life is God's gift. My grandparents and my uncle were unafraid. They had full consciousness of what they were doing."

Sazan Hoxbe: "As devout Muslims we extended our protection and humanism to the Jews. Why? Besa, friendship and the holy Koran."

Avdul Haxbiu: "My daily prayer is a prayer of peace, friendship and brotherhood. The Koran says to give to a beggar with your right hand and to do it quietly. God will know. I am a fourth member of my family to go on the hajj to Mecca."

Family of Kasem Jakup Kocerri: "I am proud to be recognized by the state of Israel as Righteous Among the Nations. We have been a family of Muslims for five hundred years. Besa came from the Koran…To save a life is to go to paradise."

Drita Veseli: "The Koran teaches us that all people – Jews, Christians, and Muslims- are under one God."

Drita Salillari: "Besa is in the Koran and that is what we live by."

Family of Ali and Nadia Kazazi: "Without Besa there is no Koran. For the heart there is no color of skin. No man or woman can forget God."

Family of Hamid and Xhemal Veseli: "Four times we opened our doors: first to the Greeks, WWI, then to Italian soldiers and Jews, and most recently to the Albanian refugees fleeing the Serbs from Kosovo. **Only the Jews showed their gratitude.**"

Family of Ramadan and Isa Nuza: "It is an Albanian tradition, then and now, always to have our door open for guests. The next time it could be our family needing shelter. We are religions Muslims and say our prayers in Arabic."

Family of Mullah Shabani: "We have been Muslims for three hundred years. My grandfather, Shoban was a mullah. My parents were just doing the right thing in sheltering the Jews. It was justice. My father was a good man, a very good man."

Albanian Muslims believe God asks them to practice **Besa;**

Jews believe God asks them to practice **Hasid;** and

Christians believe God asks them to practice **Agape Love.** When love is practiced, especially when it takes great sacrifice, people live with harmony and happiness, side by side.

Yad Vashem, the Jerusalem-based holocaust memorial, honors more than 25,000 non-Jewish rescuers of Jews during the Holocaust as Righteous among the Nations. Though most are Christian, it also includes a contingent of Muslim rescuers from Albania and nearby regions.

In Albania and Kosovo, Muslims sheltered at grave risk to themselves and their families, not only the Jews of their cities and villages, but also thousands of Jews fleeing the Gestapo from other European countries.

"Besa" by Norman Gershman, author, phtographer. Thanks to Syracruse University Press for permission to use this vital Muslim history.

More Kingdom Love
In Action
World Vision

"Beloved, if God so loved us, we ought to love one another."   *1 John 4:11 (NKJV)*

"Tena, I came to say good bye."

Tena thrust White Jade into my arms. "Her father beat her when she told them of Jesus like you said. Now she has lost everything!" she fumed. "I have no extra bed or food for her. What are you going to do about it?" In mid-June, 1948 the Rev. Bob Pierce stopped on Amoy Island heading home following a tremendously successful evangelistic tour in China. When he visited this small girls' school run by Dutch Reform Missionaries, Director, Tena Hoelkeboer requested that he talk to the girls. Still exhilarated from the months of preaching in China to thousands of poor, unhappy people who welcomed Jesus' loving message, he told the girls the gospel in simple terms. Several invited Jesus into their hearts. He requested that they tell their parents they were now Christians. En route to the airport the next morning he walked into the school where Tena handed Bob a child named White Jade.

"I stood there with the child in my arms. Tears were running down her cheeks. She was scared to death…shaking in my arms. She was heavy and my arms were getting tired. I was shaken to the core.

I had never been held accountable for any consequences of my message. Now I was faced with "Is what I say true? Is there any responsibility involved? Believe me; you do some thinking at a moment like that."[5] Bob reached into his pocket and pulled out his last $5 and laid it on the desk. With tears in his eyes, he replied, "This is all the money I have, but I promise I will send more when I get home."

From that heart-rending event, the concept for World Vision (WV), one of the world's largest Christian humanitarian organizations working against poverty, disease, hunger; and providing for orphans, was born. Bob's prayer from that day onward became "let my heart be broken by the things that break the heart of God."

Bob was unaware God was making preparation for the tragedy and devastation soon to ravage Africa by the AIDS/HIV epidemic, leaving 15 million orphans, or that WV would become a key instrument of Kingdom Love, salvaging and restoring millions of children with hope-filled lives across that continent.

Bob's daughter, Marilee Dunker wrote in her book "Man of Vision" that her father as a young man, prior to preaching in China, tried one job after another, never satisfied, but driven onward. He had several deep spiritual experiences and fortunately, married Lorraine, a preacher's daughter, who was richly endowed by belief in prayer. Bob and his wife, Lorraine empathized with the hurting, especially those who had not heard the Good News that God loves them. His testimony and preaching connected well with the listeners. When he served as a youth minister many young people accepted Jesus Christ as their Lord and Savior. Youth for Christ found his vitality, music, humor and desire for everyone worldwide to hear the Gospel, a perfect match for their organization. It was here that he met and worked with a young Billy Graham.

From that preaching trip in China, Bob wrote:

"Soochow, July 1947... Wish you and Sharon (baby daughter) could walk the mile to church with me, narrow streets, and masses of humanity everywhere. Everyone here curious about the foreigner, calling the one word they know 'Hal lo!' Look in the shops – eight

---

[5] "This One Thing I Do" by Franklin Graham

year-old boys wielding sledge hammers ten hours a day, filthy hands chopping meat, chopping vegetables, scratching open sores, back to kneading bread. Little children, naked, urinating in the streets. Every mother with child sucking a breast adorable babies. Skilled craftsmen making furniture, making metal pots, making shoes, making wicker and making clothes. Buddhist temples. Every step a rickshaw boy grunting for you to get out of the way. Every direction someone squatting with chopsticks, eating rice- Oh, I give up. It's indescribable…but I have never felt so needed in the Lord's work before."

"Hanchow, Aug. 1947 "This is God's time in China…these people are so needy and hungry for the gospel that even a nobody like me, can under God, do so much that I doubt if I'll ever be willing to just go through the motions of evangelizing in America again."

"Sian 1947

"Over 20 thousand people attended the last meeting in Sian. The Chinese were packed in like sardines…jammed in together with no aisles, No seats, no alter space, just one solid pack of hungry, ignorant, yet wonderful people. They stood attentively for two hours and fifteen minutes…at least two thousand responded to the invitation by raising their hands."

"Shanghai 1947 We had the honor of a lifetime yesterday…of being entertained by Madame Chiang Kei-shek in her home. She said …'China's greatest problem is spiritual bankruptcy'."[6]

Bob Pierce was never the same after his trips to China. He went a young man in search of religious adventure, but came home a man with a mission. He was shocked and outraged that such extreme suffering and spiritual darkness could go unchallenged. Upon arriving home he immediately set out to do something about it. Armed with movies he had taken in China, he traveled from church to church proclaiming "This is the reality for half of the world's population: hunger, sickness, filth, poverty, death, topped off by total spiritual destitution." He would close with the razor-sharp challenge that echoed within his heart, "What are you going to do about it?"

---

[6] "Man of Vision" by Marilee Pierce Dunker Most of this account of Bob Pierce has come from her book, except The White Jade story from Frankin Graham.

This tireless, worldwide Youth for Christ worker changed directions when World Vision (WV) was officially launched in Portland, Oregon, Sept. 1950 with Bob Pierce, President; Paul Meyers, Vice President; and Frank Phillips as Executive Secretary...a missionary aid organization to meet needs during times of crisis in Asia. He turned his attention to global sponsoring of orphans, training indigenous church leaders, constructing hospitals, providing aid to refugees, war and disaster victims.

When Mao came to power in China he kicked out all the missionaries and killed millions of church people, especially its leaders. Pierce went to Korea and Vietnam as groups were begging for someone to come preach to them. The Communists then invaded Korea. During the Korean War, Bob Pierce preached to service men and women from dawn to late night, often near the front lines, never afraid, just full of desire that these soldiers would hear and know that God loved them.

- He preached to Korean people and founded orphanages for the bi-racial children being left behind by our soldiers.
- He once brought 26 babies back on a plane. They were among the first Euro-Asian orphans adopted by Americans.
- The needs of the Asian people were seared into his heart as he saw how few material things they owned and how hard they worked just to survive.

Back in America he showed movies of these people and their beautiful countries and their desperate poverty. Pierce found that Americans would donate money for food, medical care and sponsoring children so that they could have clothes, food and be able to attend school. World Vision has found sponsors for more than 4,500,000 children since its founding. After the Communists marched into Korea, Bob Pierce could only go back as a reporter, not as a preacher. He reported..."The Korean war had cost 80 percent of the Christian leaders in North Korea; in Seoul they tricked 46 leaders into meeting at a church and they have not been heard from since; 3,000 Christians were murdered on the banks of the Han River, hands bound by barbed wire; and a huge pit in Korea held the bodies of 1,800 persons killed because they went to church." Bob appealed for medicinal funding aid for Korean lepers and clothes for orphan children walking in the snow. With Dick Ross' help he used Korean film footage for a moving story, "38th Parallel." The American people were brought face to face with whole cities made of cardboard and newspaper where families huddled in a feeble attempt to find shelter from the winter's cold. Thousands of dark-eyed helpless children displayed ballooning stomachs in stark contrast to their toothpick arms and legs. In 1953, money and sponsorship came pouring into the organization.

With Bob on the road most of the time, Lorraine and his two daughters stayed in touch by daily prayer. They moved to Los Angeles to be close to Lorraine's father, a source of comfort and help for the family.

One of the most traveled men in America, Bob met with leaders around the world.

Queen Wilhelmina and Queen Juliana of the Netherlands shared many of his interests. When he was able to bring Lorraine to a meeting, Queen Juliana asked her, "How do you live alone without your husband? And how do you raise your children without their father?"

Covering the Queen's hand with her own, Lorraine said, "I can do it only because the Lord enables me to do it, and He does."

Bob's schedule never slowed down as the invitations to preach and participate in World Visions' work called him to the Philippines, India, Afghanistan, The USSR, Austria, Greece, Italy and France. As Bob continued his journey of faith and saw greater needs, Tena Hoelkeboer's words would ring in his ears. "What are you going to do about it?"

Lorraine flew with Bob to the New York Billy Graham Crusade where she promptly came down with the flu and had to return home. Bob continued to meetings in Buffalo. Her health often prevented her being able to travel with him; however she did fly to Korea for World Vision's 10th Anniversary. Bob and Loraine were awarded national honors and the red carpet was rolled out for them both.

The intense work and travel caught up with Bob. World Vision's continued growth had taken a toll on Bob's body. One of his favorite jobs while directing World Vision was his weekly radio program. In 1963 the Board of Directors of World Vision cancelled his weekly broadcasts and made Dick Halverson acting president while Bob Pierce went into seclusion and complete rest.

The family went on living the best they could and prayed continually for his recovery. Months later Bob began to ease back into an active role with World Vision, concentrating his effort on film projects like "The Least Ones" and "Viet Nam Profile." Back in charge he made unhesitating responses to needs that were not being met. "That's why World Vision was created – to organize and finance the fulfillment of commitments Bob Pierce made." he said. At the start when World Vision was small, supply and demand balanced out, although not without God's miraculous intervention time and time again. As World Vision expanded, the projects became larger and sums of money grew astronomically. Millions of dollars passed through the office annually and required scrupulous accounting. World Vision began placing restrictions on Bob's authority to commit money without their voted approval as the government required detailed accounting for all funding given and how utilized.

It was a tough period for a free spirit like Bob who usually only checked with the Holy Spirit before making on-the-spot commitments. He made a film "A Cry in The Night," which was costly, and told the Board of Directors he had a 'spiritual leading' to lend the film out for free if churches and groups would pay the postal fees and take offerings for missions' projects. The leaders at World Vision did not approve. However, he insisted so two hundred copies were working around the clock all over the country. The resulting World Vision donations were the largest from any single project up until that time. However, Bob and the board remained in conflict.

When Bob came home after meeting with the board one last time he told the family, "Well, I let them have it all. I gave them everything...films, my work, my office. I started with nothing; I'll leave with nothing."

After a years' rest and some time at home, Bob became president of a small organization he could run from the heart. Bob's heart-ache for orphans abandoned during the Korean and Vietnam Wars, helped him found, in addition to World Vision, Samaritan's Purse, which he later placed into the care of Franklin Graham.

Bob and Lorraine both had health issues, but they trusted in God's unfailing provision and continuous displays of faithfulness. God walked with Bob and his family through their ups and downs, pains and sorrows and times of separation. God never removed His blessing from Bob's ministries.

After a diagnosis of leukemia, Bob would take his treatment and continue traveling and preaching. He invited the family to a special dinner on September 2, 1978. They had a wonderful evening of love and reconciliation. Their time was filled with joyous hugs, tears, laughter and prayers. When he began tiring, reluctantly they said their good byes. Bob Pierce went to be with His heavenly Father four days later.

Described as "an affair of state in the Kingdom of God" Bob Pierce's Celebration of Life Service, was attended by over 1,000 people from all parts of the world. At the service, daughter Marilee spoke, ending with "…thank you for being our parents. More than that, I thank you for being willing to be so wounded, to give so much for the Kingdom of God…You see, everybody gets hurt. Everybody suffers in this world. But so many people suffer for no reason, for nothing of lasting significance or consequence. I'm proud that what we gave was for this cause, that Jesus might be glorified. And I praise him for His faithfulness."

Like John Wesley of old who did not fear that the Methodist Church would cease to exist, but that it could eventually become a dead church, Bob Pierces' last words reflect similer concerns. "My single greatest concern is the growing inertia I see, inertia born out of our luxury and materialism. People are fooling themselves when they say the job is done. The vast body of people in the world today has never been given enough information to know if they accept or reject Jesus. Jesus commanded us to go to the uttermost parts of the earth…Most people think what the Gospel needs is more clever, skilled people, when what it needs is more people who are willing to bleed, suffer and die in a passion to see people come to Christ!"

Upon hearing that, someone whispered, "That is what Bob Pierce was all about."

Material quoted comes from the book: "Man of Vision" by Marilee Pierce Dunker. Marilee, daughter of Bob Pierce, is World Vision's Child Advocate/Advocacy and Communications coordinator. White Jade story from Franklin Graham, "This one Thing I Do."

World Vision And Bono
Join Hands Africa's
Aids/Hiv Crisis

*Blessed are you who hunger now for you will be
filled.*   *Luke 6:21 NKJV*

Daily at 6:A.M. as the dawn breaks, the massive refugee camp
begins to stir. As far as the eye can see the earth is covered
with tiny makeshift lean-tos, hastily crafted out of sticks and grass.
As the sun crests the nearby hills, people begin to queue up just
outside the World Vision compound for their daily ration of food.
In camps like Ethiopia's historic Gondar region, a strange mist – a
combination of smoke from a thousand wood fires and morning fog
– hangs over the barren hillside like a shroud.

Inside the compound, World Vision staff and volunteer helpers
move as rapidly as possible to fill the bowls of hungry men, women
and children, and wonder if there will be enough food for the large
crowd waiting outside the gate. Some stricken people have walked
over 75 miles, carrying their few belongings on their back with a
baby in their arms. Before leaving their homes, most had sold all of
their possessions to buy what little food was left in the local markets.
Now destitute, their only lifeline is the porridge and dry rations being
distributed here. In addition, orphaned little children stand in line
holding the hands of smaller brothers and sisters. These are among

a growing generation of orphans, surviving after their parents gave them the only food left- then die somewhere along the road.

In the early 80's this pain and anguish stirred deep Irish emotions of U2 rock band leader, Bono and his wife, Ali. They came to Africa to work with World Vision for a month, helping serve simple porridge meals to the eager grasping victims. They were shocked to see hundreds of people arrive daily, adding to the World Vision Famine relief centers like Ajibar, Korem, Alamiatta, Ethiopia, Chad, Darfur and many more African areas.

After receiving their rationing of water and food, people would lay down from total exhaustion. Drought drove most to wander from their homes seeking food. Many were running from the persecution of tyrants, wars, religious and tribal rivalries.. Every day they come in larger numbers; some days there is not enough food to go around. Those left hungry have the promise of being first in line the next day. Children with bellies larger than the rest of their bodies with little sticks for arms and legs cry from hunger pains. Mothers and some fathers do what little they can to comfort them.

During the 80's, this was the daily scene for months in Ethiopian feeding stations and Medical Units set up in villages.

When asked how he managed when they ran out of food and there were still many people in line who were hungry, one worker replied, "I look at those the next day who survived; glad that they are alive and we could help them. Some are so weak when they arrive that they die, whether they get food or not. I concentrate on the fact that we can save most; those who do not survive, no longer suffer, or I could not bear it."

Because refugees have various stages of starvation WV has developed differing types of food served at the Therapeutic Feeding Centers:
Within the feeding centers three types of feeding programs operate simultaneously:
   a) Super-intensive for those children on the verge of death, needing to be fed slowly. The bodies of these children have to literally be coaxed back to life; and
   b) Intensive feeding three or four times a day for children with moderate to severe malnutrition.

1) Faffa is a porridge made from wheat flour, sugar, oil and a high protein powder supplement used for rapid stabilization of severely malnourished children. It is given three or four times daily for children with moderate or severe malnutrition and in all daily meals for the malnourished;

2) Dry rations are usually sorghum, millet and /or other cereals distributed to families and individuals to take home and cook along with the other foods people may have with them.

3) General feeding once-a-day meals served at noon-time to older children and adults.

Prior to this African visit to see first hand what was occurring with starving people, Bono and his U2 Band performed in the Live AIDS London Concert to raise money for starving people. In Africa, their hunger was difficult to face but, one event stabbed Bono's heart with greater concern. A man stepped out of the feeding lines and handed a baby to Bono, who held the little one for a moment. The crying man through the help of an interpreter would not take the baby back. "You keep my child, I die soon, mama die too."

Steve Reynolds, The World Vision representative, in charge of orienting volunteers like Bono and Ali, remembers being in similar situations himself. "That kind of experience forces you to search your soul," said Reynolds. "I believe that encounter shook both Bono and Ali to their core, and made them realize this wasn't just a 30-second TV commercial. It was real and like no other human experience." That painful reality and despair impacted them both.

New volunteers always have a difficult time the first few days until they see many adults getting stronger and children beginning to smile and play again. Bono and Ali developed music and drama programs for the children who were in the center all day. The children loved 'The Girl with the Beard' – a reference to the mop-type 'mullet' hairdo that Bono was sporting at the time... and the beard he had grown while in the camp. The staff praised his energy, spirit and creativity in helping write songs about eating healthy vegetables, washing your hands before you eat, and other healthy reminders. Bono and Ali truly endeared themselves to the staff, children and families in the center. All were sad to see them go when the month ended. Though food served daily saves the hungry, Bono was haunted by babies abandoned as their parents die from starvation and AIDS.

Steve took Bono and Ali on a tour of the various camps and compounds run by different agencies working in Ethiopia at the time. They spent days in Land Cruisers, small airplanes, walking through row after row of makeshift huts where people waited for their next handout of food. Bono was tireless in his compassion. It seemed that he wanted to hold every child in Ethiopia just once and comfort every mother. One special camp they visited was the Irish Concern Agency Camp near Soddo, in Province Wdayita.

Before Bono and Ali flew back home, the staff had a party with songs and stories. It was a time of celebration after much sadness and heartbreak. For those working in Ethiopia at the time, their visit was a 'healing and uplifting moment we would all treasure.'

While saying goodbye, Bono offered to get Steve passes 'if ever you are in a city where U2 is playing.'

"Years later, when we moved to Bangkok I would hear his music and remember those days in Ethiopia with a smile. One song in particular, written about Bono's African experience, is entitled *Where the* Streets *Have No Name*. When it plays on the radio, images of Ajibar would come flooding back, the tears and the laughter all at once. That song will always remind me of Ethiopia, Steve Reynolds recalled."[7]

Bono went back to his show business life, but could not forget those little faces and their sick parents. He became a champion for the poor and downtrodden. He also visited Latin America where priests laid down their lives to defend the poor against political oppression. His song "Bullet in the Blue Sky" is a ballad about the daily struggles of peaceful villagers caught up in the violence of guerrilla warfare. In 2000, Bono became involved with the Jubilee movement – a movement to cancel Third World nations' debt. U2's concerts at times seem more like political action rallies than musical events. Since time began, God has utilized ordinary and gifted people, who hear His song of love, to improve life, especially when children are hurting.

---

[7]   Steve Reynolds, World Vision /MKTG/WVUS/World Vision June, 2008 Steve Reynolds is Director of Advocacy, Integration and Campaigns for WV

In 2005 in Louisville, KY, Bono spoke at a large event to raise HIV/AIDS awareness. Steve Reynolds was manning the booth for World Vision. Bono told his Africa story about the feeding camps and people trying to give away their most precious possessions, their children, due to AIDS and starvation. Bono mentioned how a fellow helped him understand the problems in Africa and he is with us tonight. Without him I wouldn't be here doing this. This is the guy who showed me what AIDS was doing to Africa... he is why I am here. Stand up Steve Reynolds." The band played "Where Streets Have No Names"; the crowd went wild with applause and an amazed Steve was almost too stunned to speak.

Bono learned more about the shocking impact that HIV/AIDS was having, particularly in Africa. He also learned the churches in America and Europe were doing little about it. At a speech given at the USA 2006 National Prayer Breakfast, Bono made his feelings known. "...16,500 Africans are still dying every day of a preventable disease," he told the packed crowd in Washington DC. "This is not about charity; it is about justice and equality. Because there is no way we can look at what's happening in Africa and, if we're honest, conclude that deep down, we really accept that Africans are equal to us. Anywhere else in the world, we wouldn't accept it. Look at what happened in Southwest Asia with the Tsunami. 150,000 lives lost to that misnomer of all misnomers 'mother nature.' In Africa, 150,000 lives are lost every month. A tsunami every month and it's a completely avoidable catastrophe.

It's annoying, but justice and equality are mates, aren't they? Justice always wants to hang out with equality, and equality is a real pain."[8]

Bono took up the cause of HIV and AIDS with his characteristic near maniacal energy and focus. He formed his own organization DATA (Debt, AIDS and Trade in Africa) to advocate for these in global capitols' halls of power. His concerts raise awareness of AIDS/HIV and regularly recruit voices and money to these causes.

He began talking to people from the United Nations and heads of state. Portions of his concerts' profits went to buy medicine and

---

[8]   Bono's remarks at The National Day of Prayer, 2006, Washington DC

supplies for Africans who were infected and hurting; people were encouraged to sign up for the ONE Campaign, to advocate for an even greater fight for Aids and poverty. He helps support children relief centers.

Bono is still amazed at the impact being made, especially in Africa.

Ali added her name and funds to several charitable causes most notably the Children of Chernobyl Campaign dedicated to helping families cope with the aftermath of the Chernobyl nuclear accident.

Steve Reynolds, his wife Nancy and their three children now live in the USA. He is based at the Federal Way, WA, office of World Vision, where he serves as Director of Advocacy, Integration and Campaigns.

After World Vision's current President, Rich Stearns, visited a family of AIDS orphans on his first visit overseas, he and the Board made AIDS/HIV a focus of the organization. A team was set up, funds were budgeted and World Vision's "Hope Initiative" was born to revamp and improve the organization's response to the growing global pandemic. Stearns who was formerly CEO of Lenox China, one of America's most prestigious companies, said in a recent Guideposts' article: "Corporate perks and Jaguars mean nothing after you've tasted the reward of doing the real work God always meant for you to do. In the end, words fall short. 'Follow me', says God. And when we do, we find our deepest purpose and the true adventure begins."

Recently Bono said, "It's a mind blowing concept that the God who created the universe might be looking for company, a real relationship with people."

FACTS ABOUT HIV/AIDS
THE CRUEL
WORLDWIDE KILLER

HIV/AIDS was **NOT** created by Americans in a test tube to kill other people! In America the killer known as AIDS/HIV reared its ugly head in 1960. The Soviet propaganda program "INFECTION" tried to spread the concept that HIV/AID was created in America, which, unfortunately, many still believe.

A Haitian immigrant who contracted the disease in 1959 in African Republic of Congo brought it to America. More widely known for spreading HIV/AIDS is a Flight Attendant, who in 1982 brought the disease to Canada and America as he managed to infect at least 40 victims out of the 248 who were in sexual liaisons with him or each other. HIV/AIDS was first noted among homosexual men and injection drug users who shared needles.

Active and caring people around the world are spending millions to help AIDS/HIV infected people, making a huge difference. Several African nations have reduced their nations' rates by 15%-19%.

Washington, D.C. has become the USA's highest per capita HIV/AIDS infected population. Sadly, sixty-eight percent of the infected D.C. victims are black. Doctors and leaders have begun speaking at schools to educate the younger set in hopes of cutting off this killer disease. There is little excuse for citizens living in cities where condoms and resources are available to offset AIDS/HIV, to still become infected.

In the USA for years, the numbers of AIDS/HIV victims went down, but have started back up with a vengeance. Isn't it time for sex buyers and sellers, as well as needle users to take some responsibility for their behaviors?

There are many myths about this killer, but thank God, compassionate people are fighting back; progress is being made worldwide thanks to the money, medicine, education and hands- on assistance from multitudes of people and resources.   Geneva, Switzerland is home to the United Nations AIDS/World Health Organization. Compare their 2007, 2012 and 2013 data:

	2007	2012	2013
A) Millions living with HIV	39.5	35.3	
B) Millions of newly infected people	4.3	2.3	2.1
C) Millions who died.	2.9	1.6	1.5

Fifteen million receive the antiretroviral therapy (ARTs).

The UN was gravely concerned when large portions of African female population were coming down with AIDS. They predicted there would be a worldwide heterosexual HIV/AIDS pandemic. This has not proven to be true. Outside Africa HIV/AIDS is primarily infecting male homosexuals; persons of both genders in the sex trade; and drug injectors sharing needles.

The horrible concept of "Virgin Cleansing" is rapidly spreading the HIV/AIDS in Africa as ignorant men believe that having sexual intercourse with a virgin will transfer the illness to her. Thousands of cases of this occurrence in sub-Saharan Africa are reported, where men are infecting young girls and even infants. Unfortunately, this idea did not originate in Africa. In sixteenth century Europe it was a very common myth. Social sexual diseases are not new and ignorance of their deadly impact continues to threaten human beings as they practice assorted sexual activities.[9]

---

[9]   United Nations World Health Organization HIV/AIDS Web Sites, March 2008, April 21, 2014

Dr. Peter Piot of the UN AIDS/World Health Organization says there are 4384 new infections per day. Of the infected millions in the world, 68 percent of the people live in sub-Saharan Africa. The billions spent in the past few years have seen the number of infections drop, but the long-range tragic consequences of this epidemic are 15,000,000 million orphans.[10]

When Moses wrote the first books of the Bible, God gave him directions for the Hebrews in cleanliness, health, nutrition and sexual conduct. Bathing, not touching unclean things, and burning homes, utensils and clothing from sick persons were part of the heritage that helped Jews survive since 2000 BC. Many compassionate people have difficulty believing that a loving God, would on occasion instruct the Hebrews to ' kill all the men, women, children and animals' they conquered. But unhealthy lifestyles and sexual practices among some cultures killed animals and mankind. Some still do. Hebrews were admonished to be a 'blessing to all the nations.' Could survival of the human race be one of the reasons that God's word holds strong instructions regarding His gift of sex? The average death age for active homosexuals is 42. Was God trying to save humankind from dreadful diseases and early deaths? Most other ancient people and tribes have disappeared, but the Hebrews and their particular DNA survives.

The HIV/AIDS work must continue for years to come. Unfortunately, some developing nations out of ignorance reject and deny the truth about this deadly contagion. Financing is continuing for education, medicine, supplies and workers that are stemming the tide of this man-made tragedy, thanks to insistent efforts by Bono and his U2 band, World Vision and other groups. The UN Aids World Health Organization, the United States government under George W. Bush, wealthy philanthropists like Bill Gates and many churches are working to save people, especially the children.

Churches like Ginghamsburg United Methodist Church, Tipp City, Ohio donate to stem AIDS/HIV deaths as the congregation gives fifty- percent of what they would normally spend on Christmas presents ($1.8 million) for orphanages for young victims and

---

[10] Data on AIDS/HIV history and development numbers from the UNWHO..

self-sustaining agriculture programs to train them to make a living and have hope for the future.[11]

These 15,000,000 orphans would have broken the heart of Bob Pierce just as they touched the heart of Bono, Ali and the U2 band, Rich Stearns, and millions more, who strive to bring worldwide compassionate assistance and solutions. WV has arranged for sponsorship and community care for millions of children. In 2014 WV was able to assist 10.7 million people. There is so much yet to be done; however, thank God, progress is gradually turning the HIV/AIDS plague around.

Currently World Vision, under the leadership of Rich Stearns, continues to develop programs to aid and educate the sick, build schools as well as find sponsors and community support for orphans. They work and cooperate with The United Nations, Heads of State and international churches and organizations to maximize utilization of resources.

"Whoever receives one of these little children in My name receives Me; and whoever receives Me, receives not Me, but Him who sent Me." Mark 9:37 NKJV

---

1) United Nations World Health Organization Web Sites for AIDS/HIV
2) World Vision
3) Steve Reynolds
4) UN AIDS/World Health Organization

[11] 5) "Good News" magazine July/Aug 2007 ' United Methodists Join in Sudan Water Mission Project' by Linda Bloom

WORLD VISION TURNS
SIXTY-FIVE

*"There is only one thing more costly than caring, and
that is not caring."*[12]

$\mathcal{D}$oes God have a sense of timing before major events occur?
Was it pure coincidence that Bob Pierces' broken heart led to
the founding of World Vision (WV) organizing sponsorship and com-
munity-based support for orphans… just prior to the AID'S epidemic
in Africa? HIV/AIDS created 15 million African orphans needing
medicine, sponsors, volunteers or relatives to care for them. The
original 1950's three-person WV staff grew from an emphasis on
Asia to more than 46,000 men and women serving in 100 nations.
WV reaches out to millions uprooted by droughts, tribal wars, ISIS,
multi-national disruptions over valuable minerals and oil, as well as
AIDS/HIV, tsunamis and earthquakes.

Matabo was barely six when her father died of Aids. Her mother
cared for her and two older brothers the best she could, but one night
she disappeared. She left the village of Isuto to go to South Africa
looking for work. When Matabo's brother abused her, Maninani, a
World Vision (WV) volunteer, took Matabo in, gave her food and
safety, teaching her God watches over her each night. Her brothers
quickly disappeared, so she was all alone. Each week Maninani took

---

[12] *The Devil at Noon by* Maxie Dunham

Matabo to church, gave her food and school fees. As commonly occurs, five years later her very ill mother came home and took to bed. In two months her mother died of disease and starvation. In Matabo's regional area there are 56,000 orphans being helped by trained volunteers like Maninani, who fortunately was able to find Matabo a WV sponsor. Enabled to attend school, Matabo believes when she is older she will find work and support herself. She has grown from a frightened, orphaned six-year old to a hope-filled teen-ager...thanks to a sponsor and volunteer mentor.[13]

Making sense of the chaos in Africa is difficult. World Vision (WV) began work in Uganda in 1985 when the great Ethiopian famine and tribal wars drove out vast numbers of people to seek safety and food. Over the ensuing years, 400,000 or 25 percent of Uganda's total population became displaced citizens. In early 2008 over 10,000 people were abducted. People of northern Uganda have cautiously worked for years to return to their villages and rebuild their communities. But they have done so virtually on their own, without the necessary support and resources needed to secure significant progress. Meanwhile, Uganda has cut its HIV/AIDS infections by 14 percent, in spite of these conflicts.[14]

Peace in northern Uganda will be achieved when civilians are protected and free to rebuild their communities. This requires continued political engagement, financial commitment of both natives and people dedicated to risking their own lives for the well-being of strangers. As an advocate for victims of injustice and poverty, World Vision works to empower appropriate solutions, by lobbying the United Nations (UN) and courts, while binding the wounds of the hurting.

The situations with the Sudan Darfur refugees offer especially complex problems. People like thirty-seven year old Fatama, and her seven children, came to Al Salaam South Darfur Camp. Fatama's family was attacked in her village; the militia ruthlessly killed many. She doesn't know if her husband, mother or other family members are alive. She and her children walked most of 185 miles, were picked

---

[13] World Vision Web pages March 18, 2008 www.worldvision.com

[14] United Nations' World Health AIDS Web pages March 18, 2008 www.UNAIDS. com

up by a truck that hauled 100 people over back roads, to avoiding militia shootings. They went without food for three days. Al Salaam was the last camp in Darfur still accepting refugees as the other 20 were filled to capacity. When will Fatima and her children be able to return home? Ever? Most have moved on from Darfur, but the new camps are invaded and people, especially women and children suffer mistreatment.

There are long range needs associated with helping people. Southern Sudanese voted to reestablish their independent nation in a successful election held February 2011 but no number of agreements has stopped the rebel leaders from Northern Sudan and their army, from violence against the Southern Sudanese black Africans, who own the land where the oil is plentiful. These attacks currently impact those who have been trying to return to South Sudan. This is one of the world's most severe, on-going problems, with no end in sight.

Author, Isabel Martin from Oxfam writes that this man-made crisis must have World action to prevent a catastrophe in 2015. The malnutrition is dire as 1.7 million people have fled their homes and those hiding cannot be reached by food distribution. Many, because of ethnicity, are forced to flee; they have lost loved ones, their belongings and means of livelihood. 'Food Programme' estimates that $78 million is needed to deliver assistance each month of the rainy season (May-Sept). Humanitarian food stocks pre-positioned in hard-to-reach areas have been looted or stolen. Thirteen humanitarian workers have been killed and many more wounded. Farmers can't farm as it is not safe and women and children cannot safely gather wood to cook with. The fighting continues.

However, World Vision's targeted interventions in Upper Nile have reduced severe malnutrition for very small children. Nonviolent Peace Forces have responded to widespread risks of violence by creating civilian protection teams. The UN needs to place an arms and ammunition embargo on all parties in Sudan. UNMISS needs to deploy its full mandated 12,500 troops."15

Meanwhile, World Vision, Samaritan's Purse and other non-profit groups feed, house and dig water wells for these refugees wherever they are located. They set up play centers and schools for the children, but unfortunately, it is a bleak existence of day-to-day survival with little hope. On many occasions the rebels invade these camps kidnapping and abusing children and women. This is large scale suffering by any evaluation. As thousands of South Sudanese try to move back following the successful vote for a separate South Sudan they are continually being bombed and ravaged by the rebel troops.

Like major corporations, World Vision plans, manages and evaluates the resources needed to transport tons of supplies into troubled areas via ship, air, trucks and the backs of animals. Their staffs must determine how to set up specific areas for medical care, feeding and housing without the luxury of electricity, clean water and very little flat land. Safety is always a great concern. Five truckers hauling food to the Darfur refugee camp were killed; the food and supplies were all stolen.[15]

World Vision's Kingdom love in action continues to raise the awareness of human needs by establishing campaigns for financial aid, writing letters and lobbying courts and nations. They create partnerships and understanding between people in different parts of the world enabling multi-nation cooperation.

The plight of Christian, Miriam Ibrahim in North Sudan, broke the hearts of millions worldwide. Forced to live in jail, shackled with her two year old son, she was still in irons when she gave birth to her daughter. She suffered greatly until finally permitted to live in the American Embassy, awaiting that plane trip to America, the home of her crippled husband. There are thousands who are imprisoned because they are Christians. Unfortunately, the UN focuses on *getting a peace deal, but not on securing peace.*

Thankfully, WV continually promotes affordable technologies utilizing local materials, and designs so that indigent peoples can make, use and repair wells, homes, suction water pumps, cement storage tanks and fuel efficient stoves. Personal Micro loans have become an important means of allowing impoverished people to start businesses, plant crops, build homes and schools. More than $355 million in small business loans have been made, of which 98 percent have been repaid. Self sufficiency frees people from victimhood.

---

[15] Paraphrased from World Vision Web pages March 18, 2008
15 Isabell Martin, Oxfam

This holistic approach to healthier lifestyles includes sharing God's loving offer of reconciliation through Jesus Christ, to those who wish to hear. World Vision does not coerce or demand people to convert to Christianity before, during or after receiving assistance. They work in partnership with other faith-based organizations in an effort to work collaboratively with existing community and tribal structures.

In his book, "A Hole in the Gospel" Rich Stearns, current World Vision President, recounts how a woman who had been mutilated during the Uganda attacks was receiving counseling at one of the WV facilities. She spied one of her attackers who was receiving care also. She was distraught to see one who had lopped off her ears, lips and other features, rather then kill her as she was pregnant, at this safe place of WV. With counseling and prayer, she eventually met with the young man who had come for help, haunted by what he had done to others. They forgave each other; she let him held her little boy. Spiritual healing rarely occurs with the UN Troops, armies or terrorists, but they do occur with World Vision, and the compassionate Christian groups who understand the power of Kingdom love. God has been trying to tell us for thousands of years that Kingdom love is far stronger and more enriching than hate!

To successfully carry out its mission of freeing the world's children from the tyranny of poverty, World Vision regularly monitors all their programs to ensure highest quality and efficiency. By maximizing resources, private cash gifts, government grants, and gifts-in-kind grants, a WV child sponsors' dollar results into more than a dollar in assistance to children.

At the Last Supper Jesus spoke to his disciples saying *"...I say unto you, He that believeth on me, the works that I do shall he do also; and greater works than these shall he do; because I go unto my Father. And whatsoever ye shall ask in my name that will I do, that the Father may be glorified in the Son." NKJV John 14:12-13*

Do you suppose that Jesus knew that in a single year World Vision alone would deliver?
*   4,900 semi trucks of food?
*   50,000 HIV/AIDS Caregiver Kits?

* $355,000,000 in personal small loans?
* Dig thousands of new wells for clean drinking water?
* Provide thousands of weather-proof tents in Pakistan or Darfur?
* Enlist sponsors for to pay for food, clothes and schooling for 35,000,000 orphans?

One day the number of those who love will outnumber the selfish, power-hungry and greedy. The enormous expenditures for the impoverished will instead create Kingdom living for all. Until then, World Vision continues to share, expand and reflect sacrificial and compassionate love around the world. Empowered by God's love, World Vision continues to resolve child exploitation in armed conflicts and sex trade. By energizing sponsors and resources World Vision brings hope to the hurting of the world, especially, to millions of innocent children like Matabo.

World Vision remains motivated by Bob Pierce's prayer,

"Let my heart be broken by the things that break the heart of God."

WORLD VISIONS' STATEMENT

"World Vision is a Christian relief, development and advocacy organization dedicated to working with children, families and communities to overcome poverty and injustice.

Inspired by our Christian values, we are dedicated to working with the worlds' most vulnerable people.

We serve all people regardless of religion, race, ethnicity or gender.

OUR MISSION

World Vision is an international partnership of Christians whose mission is to follow our Lord and Saviour Jesus Christ in working with the poor and oppressed to promote human transformation, seek justice and bear witness to the good news of the Kingdom of God.[16]

To Contact World Vision:
    President/Ceo Richard Stearns   Phone: 1-800 704 0830

    World vision US Programs
    P.O. Box 9716 MS 475
    Federal Way, WA 98063- 9716

    Physical Address:
    34834 Weyerhaeuser Way
    Federal Way, WA 98063

    National Office in Washington DC
    300 "I" Street Northeast
    Washington DC 20002

---

[16] World Vision Web, 2-20-2009, 3-2008 "Who We Are."

15 Isabel Martins, Oxfam GB, Oxfam House, John Smith Dr., Cowley, Oxford, OX4 2 JY, UK

EDITORIAL OPINIONS
BY THE AUTHOR

*I*n Uganda there has been ongoing fighting for many years. The civilian population has been terrorized by the rebel Lord's Resistant Army (LRA). They cut off hands ears and lips of people whom they deem sympathetic to the government. Kony, the (LRA) leader, refused to sign the negotiated peace agreement. His army continued to abduct children forcing them to become soldiers trained to kill and/or become sex slaves. His group is replaced continually by others who mistreat the vulnerable in Sudan, Democratic Republic of Congo, Central African Republic, Somalia and Ethiopia etc. These are ancestors of tribal people who sold their enemies to the Arabs, British and American slave traders with no respect for human lives, except their own. Slave trade ceased in 1830 the UK and 1865 in America. Unfortunately, several nations in Africa and Middle East still buy and sell slaves.

There is enough oil in Southern Sudan to provide an income for both the North and South. The Chinese brought in workers, but some of these jobs could be done by Sudanese locals. China's purchase of the oil could continue to supply basic income which can benefit all Sudanese. The nation can benefit from jobs in the South where oil is produced then pipelined north for shipment in Chinese ships. The world desires valuable raw minerals that Africa holds. With some negotiated management and planning, wages can be paid by putting people to work, while China and other nations acquire vital minerals, for manufacturing useful goods. Without war, Sudan could have win-win for all parties.

Unfortunately, the UN signs treaties, but fails to enforce them; the greedy, selfish and power-hungry continue to exploit African people and their mineral-rich lands, with the innocent Christians, non-Christians, Arabs, and Muslims caught in the middle.

"The power of China, who buys the oil in the northern Sudan, ensures that the oil remains theirs. They empower a Muslim Army that is stronger than the African Union or UN troops. All of the negotiated peace documents have proven to be worthless. The UN talks, but refuses to send enough troops to effect change."[17]

India provides historical proof that peaceful change can take place without ruthless exploitation and endless wars. India won independence from the UK without firing a shot. Under the leadership of Mahatma Gandhi, utilizing truth, patience and the non-violent principles of Jesus Christ, the Indian people in 30 years patiently moved from second class status into democratic freedoms. Twentieth-first century India is raising enough food for its billion and one/half people who enjoy the highest standard of living in their history. India's freedom from foreign occupation proves major tribal and national changes can be successfully negotiated without bloodshed... when God's love, truth and non-violence are permitted to prevail. Though India ranks eighth in world trade, there remains a necessity to lift their 'Untouchables', considered lower class citizens! However, many of them are receiving help from Gospel For Asia's Bridge of Hope Schools.

In spite of the improvement across the world there are still millions who lack simple vital things like latrines, clean water wells, and sufficient food and clothing.

World Vision, along with local citizens in these nations, continue to successfully attack poverty, hunger and illnesses. Because of WV and other humanitarian organizations with whom they cooperate worldwide, it is well documented the quality of life has improved for 80% of the world's poor since the 1960's. That means that the poorest

---

[17] *Surrender Is Not an Option* by John Bolton Page 358

earn $2.00 a day instead of $1.00. There is so much more to do! And as Bob Pierce would say, "What are you going to do about it?"

The updated material relating to South Sudan was from article by Isabel Martins, Oct. 2014. For more information contact: advocacy@ oxfaminternational.org or Oxfam GB, Oxfam House, John Smith Drive, Cowley, Oxford OX4 2JY, UK

LOVE WON -HATE LOST

*N*ever before in the world's history has an oppressed nation won freedom from their conquerors without armies and guns, until Mahatma Gandhi and his followers sent the British back to Europe. This tiny, prayerful man wearing skimpy clothes engineered the unique feat of turning the worlds' most important nation on its heel without firing a shot. Successful removal of the British hold on India occurred because Mahatma Gandhi taught the Indian people to apply New Testament principals of truth, love and non-violence. Though the British occupied India for over 200 years, they agreed to restore India's full independence by extracting their army and governing leaders in 1947.

Mahatma Gandhi, the architect of peace was born in 1869 into a well educated, upper level Indian, Hindu family. The very intelligent Gandhi earned his law degrees at the University of London. Seeking opportunities free of British rule, at the age of 37 he went to South Africa to practice law in 1906, amid the established Indian population. Dark skinned, he was discriminated against like the African blacks. Once he was thrown off the train, though he had purchased a first class ticket. Constant physical and racial abuses to Indian workers fueled Gandhi's efforts to seek equal treatment for them by both the white British and Dutch settlers. During the South African Boar War, Indians were not wanted as soldiers by either side.

Gandhi formed troops that manned the ambulances and nursed the sick. However, mistreatment of Indian employees continued.

Gandhi and others using civil non-cooperation, frequently brought the nation's industries to a halt. They were effective in obtaining improved working conditions, decent wages and integration for Indians. A surprised Gandhi was pulled from jail to meet with South African Prime Minister, Jan Christian Smuts, to learn that new laws removed Indian restrictions. Truth and love coupled with nonviolence had succeeded!

Gandhi observed, "Poverty is the worst form of violence," in 1914 when he, his wife and children moved back to his native India. He was distressed how under British rule, his Indian people were discouraged, in dire poverty, and unable make decent wages. Villages were filthy; people were sick and without medical care. Food was so limited men who worked hard were starving.

When he stepped onto the scene, the movement for independence from British rule was underground. It manifested itself in bombs and assassinations with a sullen hate. "...Gandhi brought all this festering hate and intrigue to the surface. He made the movement for independence open and nonviolent."

At first he met resistance with his own family and friends, but in time they understood and trusted him because he was brutally honest and fair. He had a vision for his nation to become independent, rather than remain a colony of second class citizens. He became Leader of the Indian National Congress in 1921. Leaders began working with him as they achieved successes one at a time. Thousands of Indians stood in line in the sun and rain at places they were forbidden to enter. They protested police brutality with nonviolence; they lost jobs, were beaten, and went to jail, but did not fight back. They marched hundreds of miles to the sea, making their own salt, to avoid the "Salt Tax." They were kind and loving to their foreign rulers.

His ideas of peaceful non-violence came from a hymn, "But it was the New Testament that fixed it in my heart," says Gandhi. "The Sermon on the Mount went straight to my heart. The verses, 'But I say unto you, that ye resist not evil; but whosoever shall smite thee on the right check, turn to him the other also. And if any man takes away the coat, let him have they cloak also,' delighted me beyond measure."[18]

Two primary concepts fueled Gandhi's leadership of the Indian people:

Satyagraha and Ahimisa:

1) Satyagraha: The world rests upon the bedrock of Satya or Truth. Truth means that which is. And Truth being 'that which is' can never be destroyed.

Asatya, meaning Untruth, also means 'non-existent.' If untruth does not so much as exist, its victory is out of the question.

2) Ahimisa: Total nonviolence is espoused by God's love and truth; the God of all people, Hindus, Muslims, Buddhists, Jews, Christians, Sikhs et al.

Employing civil disobedience the East Indian people went to British jails peacefully. "The jails became training schools for leadership in the new India. Almost all turned to the study of religion and prayer. 'We came out better men than when we went into jail.' You shut up people in jails only to deepen their spiritual life and broaden their mental outlook and prepare them for moral and political leadership. The jails became schools that molded character."

Gandhi summed up issues, Dec. 4, 1932 after one of his famous fasts..."Those who have to bring about radical changes in human conditions and surroundings cannot do it except by raising ferment in society. There are two methods of doing this, violent and nonviolent. Violent pressure is felt on the physical being, and it degrades him who used it as it depresses the victim, but the nonviolent pressure exerted through self-suffering, as by fasting, works in an entirely different way. It touches not the physical body, but it touches and strengthens the moral fiber of those against whom it is directed."

India's business systems broke down on strike days; nobody would work. No buses ran; no police, no teachers, no restaurants and no one came to serve at official banquets. At every meeting with the British Viceroys Indian leaders like Jawaharlal Nehru pressed the idea of freedom and an independent India

---

[18] Matthew 5: 39-40 KJ

Gandhi and Christian Conflicts

Gandhi remained true to the teachings of Hinduism, though he based his successful battle plans on Christian values. E. Stanley Jones, Methodist Missionary and friend, urged him to show both India and the West his clear-cut witness to Jesus' principals of non-violence and truth. Gandhi in gentle tears replied, "I wish I could do it. But the time isn't ripe for me to try it. I must demonstrate the power of nonviolence here in India." When urged to go to Europe to help bring peace, prior to WWII, he replied, "I have not demonstrated peace yet in my country; how can I preach it to Europe?"

Deep conflicts between the Christian Missionaries and Gandhi needed resolution. They were based on two major obstacles: 1) Eastern Indian's assumptions that all Western Christian Missionaries would naturally favor English rule, because the British were Christians and both spoke the same language; and

2) In their drive for independence, Indian Hindu's feared that massive evangelistic services, where large numbers of Indian people converted to Christianity, threatened Hindu Rule. Christians could eventually dominate the number of allotted legislative seats based on the census of Hindus, Muslims, Buddhists, Christians, and Sikhs.

However, the Christian Missionaries supported a free India. They pledged to work at healing the sick, schools and education, food supplies, and medical clinics because people desperately needed them. Individuals would be taken into the Christian Church when their spiritual change justified the outer change. Thus they removed the main bones of contention between Hindu leaders and Christians. Gandhi wrote "Though I took a path my Christian friends had not intended for me, I have remained ever indebted to them for the religious quest they awakened in me. I shall always cherish the memory of their contact. The years that followed had more, not less of sweet contacts in store for me. The system can change, but the Savior cannot."

Love, Truth and Nonviolence Are Spiritual

Gandhi understood truth and nonviolence; one was the fact and the other the method of applying the fact. He felt himself the agent of cosmic forces working through him. Gandhi accepted the law of nonviolence as rigid and as certain as the law that governs the fall of Newton's apple. He constantly worked to keep alive the people's trust in nonviolence and truth. By restoring truth and love to the status of ultimate realities Gandhi brought about a revolution in contemporary world thought. In the process India began shedding fears, hope sprang up and the light of freedom came into dull eyes as chains from centuries began to fall off.

Gandhi cut across a great deal that goes under the form of Christian civilization, and went point-blank against both war and communism. "War and communism both will use any means that gets them to their respective goals. Deceit, treachery, trickery, lies, even butchery, will be used if they can be used for the supposed right ends."

Jawaharlal Nehru considered Mahatma Gandhi's the greatest contributions to be: "Means and ends must be consistent; and what is good for individuals is also good for the nation." Gandhi's weapons were simple. He told the British authorities, "We will match our capacity to suffer against your capacity to inflict the suffering, our soul force against your physical force. We will not hate you, but we will not obey you. Do what you like; we will wear you down by our capacity to suffer. And in winning freedom we will so appeal to your heart and conscience that we will win you. So ours will be a double victory, we will win our freedom and our captors in the process."

Reporters from the West were amazed to see the Indian people taking British government punishment year after year and not return blows. If any resorted to violent reactions, Gandhi would fast again for those who had strayed from the narrow way of nonviolence. He fought on two fronts – against the British imperial power and his followers who might do violence. "They must not expect the struggles to close quickly. Time runs always in favor of the sufferer, for the simple reason that tyranny becomes more and more exposed as it is continued." The Mahatma knew that he was the stronger for acknowledging his mistakes and those of his followers.

"The country will have gained by my humiliation and confession of error. I lay claim to no superhuman powers. I wear the same corruptible flesh as the weakest of my fellow beings wear, and am therefore, as liable to err as any."

India, once the richest area in the world, was under British rule since 1757 when the British East India Company controlled most of its provinces or had compatible relations with the various state leaders. The British Crown ruled India from 1857-1947. People were exploited, much was done badly, but the British also brought modern health with small pox vaccines, the end of child brides and the suttee[19]. Gradually they had given more freedoms to the upper level Indians. Gandhi wanted Swaraj…Indian independence, no more Suzerainty[20] with the crown.

Gandhi demanded nonviolence in thought as well as outward actions, knowing that Satyagraha and Ahimsa of the brave are always superior to armed resistance. "This can only be effectively proved by demonstration, not by argument. The sword of the Satyagrahi is love and the unshakable firmness that comes from it. A Satyagrahi must always be ready to die with a smile on his face, without retaliation and without rancor in his heart."

When requested not to begin nonviolent civil disobedience he replied, "May I assure you I shall not embark on civil disobedience without copious praying. You have, perhaps, no notion of the wrong that this government (British) has done and is still doing to the vital part of our being. But I must not argue. I invite you to pray with and for me.

Passive resistance is an all-sided sword; it can be used any how; it blesses him who uses it and also against whom it is used, without drawing a drop of blood."

Behind these gentle words there was a determination of steel…He felt he was an instrument of God for a world situation and some day his method would be needed in world affairs. "…It may be long before the law of love will be recognized in international affairs. Yet if only we watched the latest developments in Europe and Eastern Asia with an eye to essentials, we could see how the world is moving steadily to realize that between nation and nation, as between man and man, force has failed to solve problems."

Mahatma Gandhi and the loyal Indian people needed thirty years to win India's and Pakistans' independence by nonviolent means. Gandhi

---

[19] Burning of widows on a pyre (death fire) when their husband died.

[20] A situation where a nation controls another nation, but allows domestic sovereignty.

insisted that the separate nation of Pakistan be formed for Muslims so they could live under their beliefs, not those of the Hindus. Pakistan was then halved to form Bangladesh. Sadly the friction between Muslim Pakistan and India dims the relationship of those nations. The British rulers kept Pakistani tribesmen quiet by force, subsidy, or bribery. Today problems of peace between India and Pakistan are still sensitive.

Gandhi, the Conscience of Mankind

Gandhi spent years criticizing the system of missions and methods of Christians, but in the end he furthered the cause of Christ. The man who was most critical turned out to be constructive at the place it counted.

A serious problem Gandhi had not resolved was the subservient role of the Dalits (Untouchables) whom Gandhi wanted released from their demeaning role in Indian life. His simple dress and lifestyle were adapted to identify with downtrodden and outcast people. However, the Father of India, lovingly called Bapu, achieved his main goal of India's independence. Gandhi's Oct. 2 Birthday is an Indian National Holiday. Long considered backward and unable to feed itself, India rose in freedom to become the world's eighth economic power. The freedoms established by India's independence, inspire 1 ½ billion citizens as they move upward from abject poverty to plenty.

The world's leaders and citizens can learn from this humble man who said, "The ways of truth and love have always won...I will die for them, but I will not kill for them." During Gandhi's era sophisticated Westerners made fun of the little guy who wore a loin cloth, spun wool, fasted and prayed. But spiritually strong Gandhi succeeded in doing what no other leader in the history of the world has done—inspire a country to achieve independence from an occupying nation through truth, love and peace. Impossible you say, and the world would agree with you, but Gandhi proved how truth and nonviolence are far more powerful in practice then oppression, hate and wars.

Gandhi taught that fasts were not to be used for personal gain. They fasted for killing of policemen, for riots or assorted misbehavior of Hindus and British, never for personal gain. Examples include: a 3-day fast that settled Ahmadbad Mill Workers dispute; 1932 Fast permitted

The Untouchables a high proportion of legislative seats; and the 1935 fast for two boys' immoral acts, taking their sins upon himself. The fasts helped his people to retain their nonviolent, non-cooperative attitudes. Step by step, fast by fast, laws improved and the British agreed to India's full independence.

Sadly, in January 1948, Mahatma Gandhi was on his way to a large New Delhi prayer meeting when a man opposed to his ideas, fired point-blank shots into his breast. Three gun shots ended Gandhi's wise leadership of a 30-year, nonviolent war that freed India from the world's mightiest power.

US President Abraham Lincoln was shot for the same reason that Gandhi was killed, namely, for the crime of wanting to heal the wounds of a divided nation. Secretary Stanton said as he stood beside the dead leader, "Now he belongs to the ages." It was also said of Mahatma Gandhi, "Now he belongs to the ages, for if there are to be any ages to come for man on this earth, we will have to apply Christ's truth and nonviolence."

Not just India, but the entire world learned how the application of these powerful truths impact those who practice them as well as those who are recipients.

Since the death of Gandhi, the late Dr. Martin Luther King and Nelson Mandela have put truth and nonviolence in action, bringing citizens into equality status in all tiers of life.

This tiny architect of peace had returned to his nation to find an India in fear; he left it free and independent.

"Love suffers long and is kind; love does not envy; love does not parade itself; it is not puffed up; does not behave rudely; does not seek its own; is not provoked; thinks no evil, does not rejoice in iniquity, but rejoices in the truth; bears all things, believes all things, hopes all things, endures all things." [21]

---

[21] 1 Corinthians: 13: 4-7 NKJV
Mahatma Gandhi, an Interpretation, by E. Stanley Jones, Methodist Missionary
My Experiment with Truth by Mahatma Gandhi

Photos

The Salvation Army

General William Booth and son Bramwell, who succeeded
him as the 2nd General of The Salvation Army
in England, near 1900.

Catherine Booth circa 1880 wearing
The Salvation Army uniform and
bonnet she designed for the women

Evangeline Booth dressed for the Alaska Gold Rush ministry. With eight Salvation Army Corp men and women,
she climbed the Chilcoot Pass and canoed across Lawson
Lake to feed 300 gold miners Thanksgiving Dinner.

Around 1925 The Salvation Army's Seattle
Washington Corp Brass Band was ready to
play and march

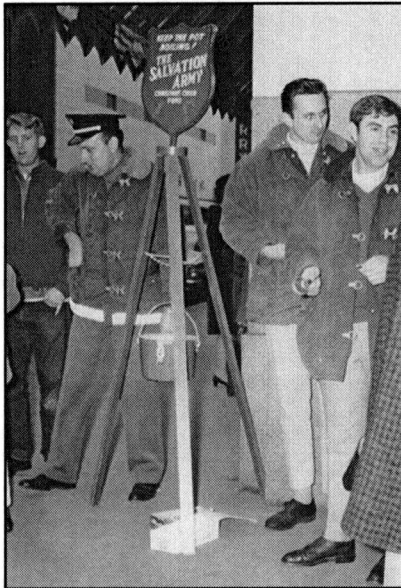

Several young men assist with bell ringing
during the 1960's as they suggest "Keep the
pot boiling! The Salvation army,
Christmas Cheer Fund.

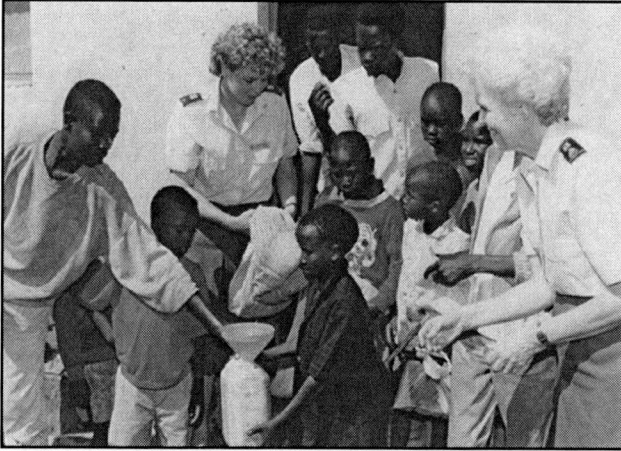

Lisa Smith and Comm. Kay Rader help children after the
1994 genocide in Rwanda, 1994.

World Vision

World Vision founder Bob Pierce stands with Korean children's
choir after a dedication of their program.

Rock star Bono of U-2 Band plays with a child
in Ethiopia in 1985 where he learned how
hunger and HIV/AIDS were destroying lives of
people of all ages.

Steve Reynolds, World Vision guide in 1985 for Bono in
Africa, meet again in 2002 during the ONE campaign in
the Heart of America.

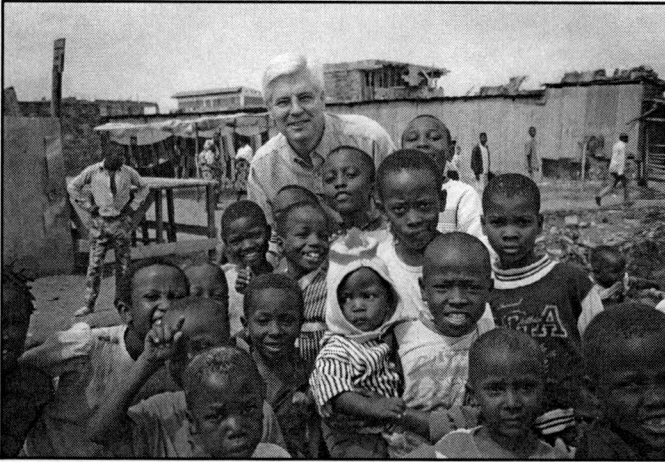

Rich Stearns, President of World Vision US, shares some smiles
with children of the streets in rural African village.

Middle East children with Rich Stearns as they
receive school backpacks.

South Africa in 2014 Dorothy Monde and neighbors complete a
borehole for clean water for their Tryroll community.

Lorraine Pierce and the three girls enjoy some time
with Bob when he was in the US between trips abroad.

Herbert Hoover

"Commission for Relief in Belgium ship with painted signs alerting German U-Boats and British Fleet not to destroy this humanitarian shipment of food. " No troops or arms are on board." These ships feed over 9 million people for four years

Belgium School children being fed at School during WWI by foods shipped in from Australia, Canada, and the USA. Herbert Hoover insisted that each child must have a hot lunch at school each day.

"President Herbert Hoover in Newberg, Oregon 1955
for the dedication of the Hoover-Minthorn House,
accompanied by State Senator Mark Hatfield and
Governor Elect, Elmo Smith."

"Nine year old, orphan, Herbert Hoover rode via train
from Iowa to live in Newberg, Oregon with his uncle
Henry Minthorn MD. He is age 11 in this photo."

Wycliffe

John Wycliffe, the 'Morning Star' of the reformation, believed that if people could read the Bible for their self they could communicate with God, find His grace, forgiveness and joy.

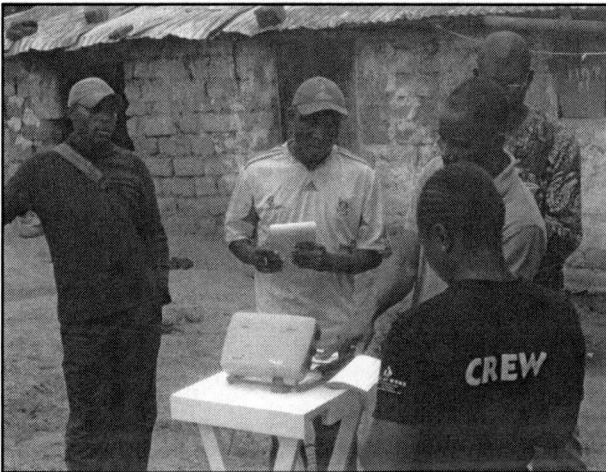

Local translator works with computer translating the Bible in African nation. Wycliffe has partners in most African nations who are translating into their own dialect and language.

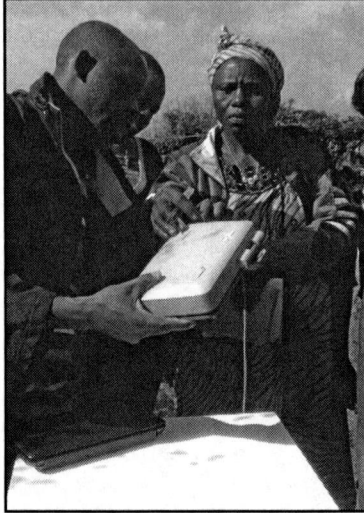

Translators hand a brand new Bible to lady who has
waited patiently for her very own Bible in her very
own language. Because 396 new Bible Translation
Acceleration Kits, now in 40 nations are in use the
time to translate has been reduced by years.

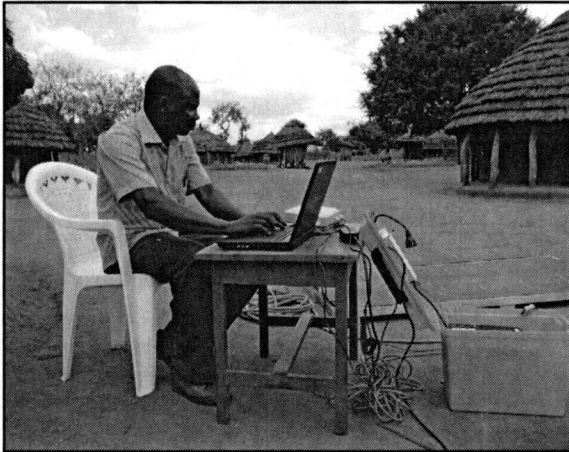

Technician works on computer at one of the 85 worldwide
centers where 2195 New Testaments are in progress and
1.329 have been completed. That means only 4,700 more to
go for all people to have God's word in their own language
or dialect. Your financial gifts can speed up the time needed.
See addresses at end of this chapter.

Medical Teams International

Ron Post, founder and long time President and CEO,
Medical Teams International felt called to help
Cambodian Refugees and then Mexico City after
the earthquake until the MTI is now a large business
sending needed medial teams around the world.

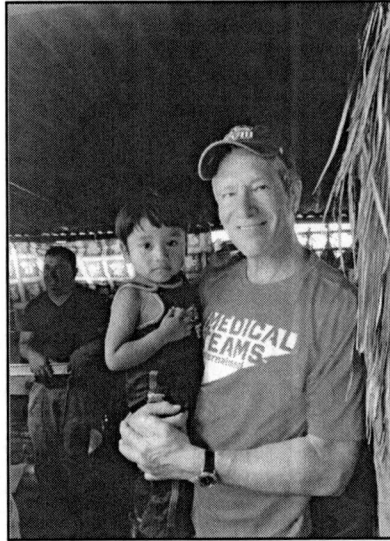

Current President/CEO Jeff Pinnero visits
Guatemala following a severe earthquake.
He has been on board since 2010.

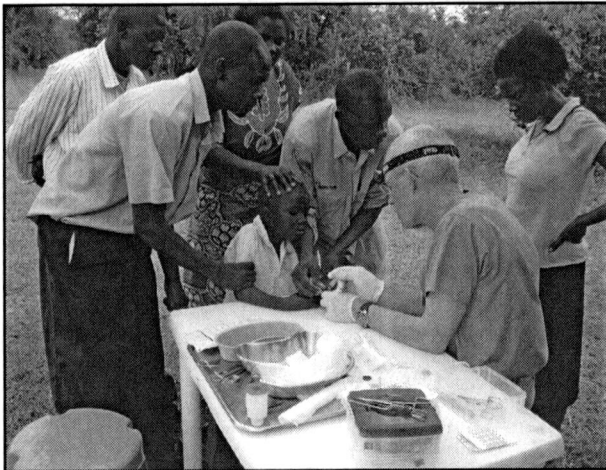

Dr. Randy Jacobs at the UN Health Care Center, Nakivale
refugee camp in SW Uganda treats a young boy. He
mentioned that they were caring for about 30,000 newly
arrived refugees from Republic of Congo and were able in
their 4 week assignment to treat 4,000+.

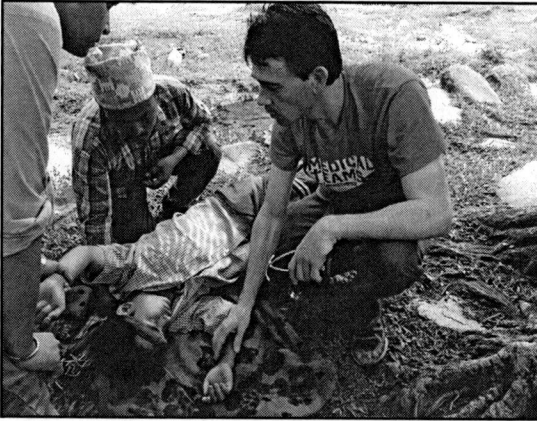

Paul helps a young boy suffering from heatstroke.

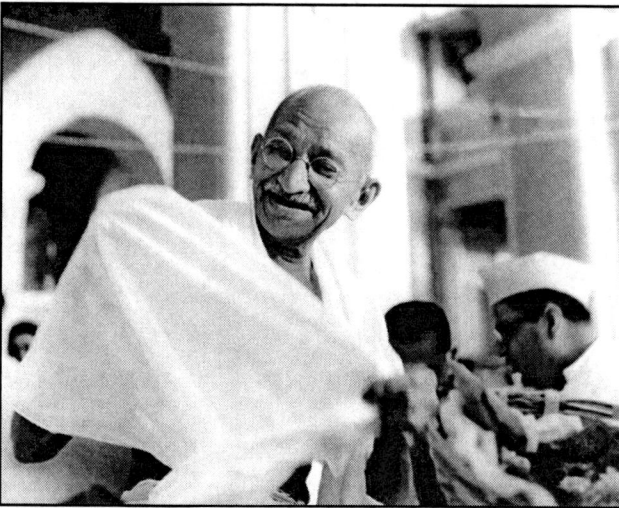

Mahatma Gandhi led the Indian people in a 30-year non-violent pro-
test against the occupying British who left peacefully in 1947. India has
since come into the eighth place economically in the world, growing
enough food for its 1 ½ billion people. They still have to eliminate poverty for many of the very lowest class, who are better off than they have
ever been. He was able to prove there are better ways than killing and
bloodshed to solve deep problems·

Gospel For Asia Leaves Stale Christianity Behind!

One day a Gospel For Asia, Christian minister reaching out in a distant village found a women named Kanga, sobbing under a mango tree. She had just been told her cancer was inoperable and she had only a few weeks to live. A good Hindu she prayed to her gods for years and now was crying out against death. Who would care for her children?

The minister shared with her. "I am from the Low Caste, yet Jesus healed my blindness and gave me the opportunity to go to school. He can heal you Kanga, if you accept Him as your God. There is only one God, not many false gods as we have been taught."

Taught by a Gospel for Asia (GFA) minister, this Hindu Dalit man came to believe in Jesus when his blindness was healed completely. He and his family became Christians and he became a student and active missionary

Kanga followed him to his church so he could pray for her. "If I am well in ten days, I will renounce the many Hindu gods and follow Jesus." In ten days, totally healed and elated, she visited her family who tossed her out. Her friends were abusive and said, "Now you are Low Caste because you believe in this Jesus!" Kanga accepted the love of her new found church friends and she too, became a missionary for the Lord. Gradually, some of her friends and family have become believers also.

Miracles occur continuously in India. One boy was dying from malaria after all his brothers died. The doctor told his parents that he had a day or two at the most. The parents in desperation went to the local Christian church where the pastor prayed for the boy several times. He was healed in a couple of days. The whole family converted. A young girl who was healed 'because of your prayers' now 'feels happy,' choosing not to commit suicide. Female suicides are common by women from the lower castes until they learn Jesus loves them too; they are included in Kingdom love.

Perhaps with all these miracles and the large population yet to hear the gospel, one can understand K.P.Yohannan, President and founder of Gospel For Asia (GAF) as he presses hard to reach American and Canadian churches with compelling urgency. A quiet man in wire-rimmed glasses with a wispy, graying beard, KP eagerly shares GAF's dreams for reaching the three billion un-churched peoples in India and Asia. In his soft voice, he tells the congregations about the multitudes of miracles taking place every day in India and Asia. The GFA seminaries train 3,000 ministers and missionaries annually and currently sponsor over 17,000 native Christian ministers and women's teams. They walk miles, climb mountains, ride bicycles, and utilize a few vans, small generators and Bibles, reaching rural villages. These young ministers are founding new Churches, as well as Bridge of Hope Schools. They drill thousands of Jesus Wells for fresh water with a goal of 2,000 per year. Four hundred GFA teams take the Indian versions of "The Jesus" film" to remote villages where hundreds are converted by hearing and seeing the gripping gospel story of God's love in their own languages and dialects.

K.P. gives genuine thanks to audiences for their prayers and financial help and asks for continuation and if possible, increased giving to buy vans for the new women's teams who travel to villages, meeting with ladies in their homes. Male pastors cannot meet with women in their homes.

KP is an unlikely candidate to be the leader for the Christian Church across India.

The scrawny, youngest of six sons, KP was his mother's last hope that one of her boys would preach to the lost in India. He knew he did have faith in Jesus, but the idea of speaking in public frightened him. At sixteen, his heart was deeply stirred when he learned of the stoning and beatings that gospel teams received in northern India as they preached about Jesus, the Christ. At a Bangalore conference, he heard George Verwer, who challenged the group to radical discipleship for the lost of the world, especially in Asia where billions have not heard the good news.

That night as K.P. prayed, his room filled with a sense of love and he felt the presence of God. "Lord God, I'll give myself to speak for You – but help me to know that You are with me." The following morning the whole world looked different as he walked the streets and observed children, cows, pigs, and vendors with baskets of food. He loved them all in a supernatural way. It was as if God had removed KP's eyes and replaced them with His, permitting KP to appreciate the lost and needy. Next thing he knew KP jumped on a high rock at the bus stop, and with heart pounding and nearly unable to breathe, he began singing a song. People stopped to watch and then God took over filling his mouth with words of His love. K.P. preached the gospel to the poor with authority and power as if God had given him a superhuman boldness. Thus in 1966 one of India's modern evangelistic missionary program, Gospel For Asia (GFA), was born.

Usually it takes a minimum of $50,000 to $70,000 a year to support missionaries from America or Canada. GFA-trained young missionaries are paid $1500 to $3500 a year in financial support as they preach to un-reached areas in India and Asia. They move to villages, planting churches, often accepting hunger, abuse, and rejection. They patiently tell the 'old, old story of Jesus and His love.' Through miracles, children's schools, healings, and conversions, villagers are filled with God's hope!

Most GFA missionaries come from their local area talking their own dialect, living the culture of their own tribe. Native Churches can place up to16 missionaries in the field for the cost of sending one from America or Canada. Releasing control of administration and trusting the native Christian methodology was difficult for many church organizations, like the first time you gave the car keys to your 16-year old. The bribery culture of some nations prompted westerners to think nationals cannot manage 'like we do.' However, native

Christian brothers and sisters, who have never lived affluently, excel in frugal and fruitful ministries.

Indigenous GFA pastors experience the Holy Spirit as high numbers of miraculous healings from illnesses, demon possession, and addictions occur while people give their hearts to Jesus and repent of their sins. Like the Wesleys, GFA plants fellowships and churches which in turn yield more spiritual fruit in disciples!

To appreciate these miracles, especially where the 'Low Caste', 'untouchables' or 'Dalits' are concerned, it helps to understand the caste system of India's Hindu religion. "Hindu creation legend states that a super being birthed the four acceptable classes of Indians: The holy men and teachers called 'Brahmans' are the top, birthed from the creator being's mouth. They are followed in status by the ruler and warrior caste called 'Kshatriyas' who were birthed supposedly in the arms of the super being. The merchant caste called 'Vaisyas' come from the thighs of the super creator and the 'Sudras' or working caste from the feet. None of the castes are to intermarry. Only the four castes birthed out of the super being are considered people. The Hindu class system declares that Dalits, Low Caste or untouchables are unlike the other four castes in that they have no karma and are considered slaves thus it has been for three thousand years. Dalits are sentenced to the most menial work and are forbidden to drink at the same wells as the other Hindus. All the castes can be reincarnated except the Dalits who just die, as they are not considered to have a soul. Thus they do all the dirtiest work of cleaning sewers, cremating bodies, disposing of dead bodies and tanning leather hides. If they become successful, mobs often burn their homes. The police turn a blind eye to common acts against them like rape, murder, and torture. However with the Christian teachings, even Dalits are learning that Jesus loves them giving them hope. (2)

A Dalit 'witch' was feared in her village, until she was healed of demon possession. Her remarkable change after accepting Jesus' healing and forgiveness encouraged her whole village to follow suit. Spiritually energized, within three years the people have built two churches; a Bridge of Hope School and drilled Fresh Water Wells for clean healthy water. The children come to the well each morning to brush their teeth and even wash off before school starts. Women no longer walk an hour to a stream for impure, germ-laden water. People love this former witch as she shares God's love. The role of the Dalit is changing as they become educated Christians.

From the very beginning of Christ's time His message was spread on earth by missionaries, most of whom were poor. The apostles were fishermen, farmers, a tax collector (much despised) and uneducated, except Judas Iscariot.

K.P. Yohannan tells of an Anglo missionary to India, who upon arrival to a small village was taken to the best house in town, made of mud and thatch. They found a beat up chair and placed it for the visitor on the mat on the dirt floor. One old man sat on the floor and watched, not saying a word. The visitor got down beside the old man and the others to tell of Jesus and His love for them. The old man was deeply impressed. He said, "I knew when he got down by me, looked me in the eyes and did not think he was better than me, he meant it when he said we are all children of God." (3)

Early in His career Jesus gave instructions when he sent out the twelve disciples, then another seventy disciples to tell the story that God wanted all mankind reconciled to Himself.

> *"He called the twelve and began to send them out two by two, and gave them authority over the unclean spirits. He ordered them to take nothing for their journey except a staff; no bread, no bag, no money in their belts; but to wear sandals and not to put on two tunics. He said to them' Wherever you enter a house, stay there until you leave the place. If any place will not welcome you and they refuse to hear you, as your leave, shake off the dust that is on your feet as a testimony against them.' So they went out and proclaimed that all should repent. And they cast out many demons, and anointed with oil many who were sick and cured them."* Mark 6:7 NKJV

When the young, newly trained K.P. Yohannan joined with a team of twelve to reach northern India they worked hard, were often stoned and beaten, but they made new converts. However, K.P. Yohannan revisited these cities where they had preached and baptized people. They had not planted churches. Christians were non-existent. It was totally secular. The schools or hospitals that had been founded by organizations still existed, but not in the name of Jesus. K.P. realized that Christians cannot just convert and leave; they must plant churches in every village.

Currently GFA supports trained missionaries and several seminaries. Every cent donated to support ministers, schools, to build churches or drill wells goes directly to that project.

In the early years when money was short or late in coming to pay the native pastors, K.P. was tempted to borrow from funds to pay them, but resisted the temptation. At the last minute when the cupboards were bare and the need was great, unexpected checks would arrive for the amount needed. He and his lovely wife, Gisela, learned to trust and wait upon the Lord. Miraculous responses to GFA needs came again and again.

This trust pattern is repeated in all successful missionary, evangelistic and benevolent organizations doing the Lord's work.

After years of productive work and success, it is not unusual for K.P. to say to his American and Canadian audiences: "Today I am calling upon Christians in the west to use weapons of spiritual warfare and advance against the enemy. We must stop skipping over the verses which read, 'If any man will come after me, let him deny himself, and take up his cross, and, follow me' and 'So likewise, whosoever of you that forsaketh not all that he hath, he cannot be my disciple.' Today I am calling upon Christians in the west to give up their stale Christianity." (1)

Thanks to ministries like GFA, Christianity, not Islam, is the fastest growing religion in the world, estimated at 125,000 new Christians per week as many signs, wonders and miracles occur regularly. India's' people receive Kingdom Love and the Holy Spirit through ministers who love and serve God, and they in turn love and serve, their brothers and sisters.

(1), (3) *Revolution In World Missions* by K.P. Yohannan, printed by Gospel For Asia
(2) *Freedom Cry* by John Gilman, printed by Dayspring Scriptures

Quotations from Mark and Luke from NKJV

Contact Information:

President/CEO K.P. Yohannan

Gospel For Asia USA
1116 St. Thomas Way
Wills Point, Texas 75169

E-mail: www.gfa.org/resource
donorservices@gfa.org

AMERICAN SCAPEGOAT- HERO

"When there is a lack of honor in government, the morals of the whole people are poisoned. There is no such thing as a no-man's land between honesty and dishonesty.

Our strength lies in spiritual concepts. It lies in public sensitiveness to evil. Our greatest danger is not from invasion by foreign armies. Our dangers are that we may commit suicide from within by complaisance with evil or by public tolerance of scandalous behavior."[22]

Germany's Kaiser Wilhelm started World War I (WWI) by invading Austria, France and Belgium in 1914. Seven million Belgium's and two million Northern French people were left starving after German troops confiscated their crops and animals. Belgium imported 80 percent of its food, but German u-boats and the British navel blockade, stopped all shipments from any source.

A multimillionaire by 1913, Herbert Hoover lived in London with his charming wife, Lou and two sons. Hoover, the "Bill Gates" of his day, in cooperation with the Belgium officials, formed the Committee for Belgium Relief (CRB). He was located where he was needed during WWI, allowing him to save nine million Europeans from starvation. Hoover and Lou asked friends around the world for help, working and traveling tirelessly, recruiting volunteer leaders and funds. He then devised the world's largest, most sophisticated relief program prompted by Northern France and Belgium's desolation.

---

[22] Herbert Hoover

Talking directly to both England's Prime Minister and Germany's Kaiser Wilhelm, he exerted keen pressures for peaceful transport of food in large Red-Cross/Relief marked ships. Agreeing these ships would not carry arms, Hoover obtained consent that neither Germany nor Great Britain would fire upon, nor permit the u-boats to torpedo, the mercy ships. In over four years of shipping, the (CRB) managed to feed all of Belgium and Northern France losing only one of shipload of food to torpedoes.

Ships picked up food in Australia, Canada and the USA, taking it to The Netherlands, where it was sent by barge up the canals to Belgium. Nine regions each had their own crews and leaders. People in each town and village were counted before carts or boats hauled food to their receiving stations. Those who could pay did, and those who could not, paid nothing. At Hoover's insistence children were provided hot lunch programs, schooling and safety.

This well executed plan resembles Jesus' example when He asked the disciples to divide the people into groups before distributing the loaves and fishes. All were fed. There were no riots. Humanitarian organizations still utilize his CBR List of Basic Necessities: 1) Funds, 2) Supplies, 3) Transportation to area and trans-shipment within territory, 4) Storage, 5) Equitable distribution, 6) Preparation, 7) Engagement of local population in distribution and management, 8) Acceptability, 9) Political acumen, 10) Moral influence, 11) Mechanisms, and 12) Continue until it is finished.

Flour was shipped in cotton sacks which in turn women and children in Belgium embroidered and sold to raise funds for food relief and to buy the release of husbands and sons from German prisoner of war camps.

Herbert Hoover's lifelong sensitivity for the welfare of children was impacted by being orphaned at a young age. Following his father's death in 1880 then his mothers' death in 1883, nine year old, 'Bertie' was taken in by various relatives. His uncle, Dr. Henry Minthorn, invited Iowan nephew, Bertie Hoover, to live in Newberg, Oregon, following the tragic death of his own son. Dr. and Mrs. Minthorn were deeply involved with Friends' Pacific Academy, the forerunner to George Fox University. Shy Bertie was expected to have wood ready for the kitchen stove daily, help Dr. Minthorn with the horses and buggy, and study hard. The Quaker Faith and work ethics resonated with his serious mind and heart.

Dr. Minthorn moved to Salem, OR to become Superintendent of the Chemawa Indian School as well as continue his medical practice and head The Oregon Land Company. Bert, now his office clerk by day, finished high school at night. A visiting engineer impressed the values of college education on this bright young man. Hoover saved his money, enabling him to enroll at age 17, in the first Stanford University freshman class, October 1891. He worked his way through college by typing, operating a laundry and delivering newspapers. Upon graduation he worked for some successful international mining companies with whom he invested his earnings.

After WWI ended, the Hoovers returned to America where he became the USA Food Administrator, Director General of the European Children's Fund, and President of the American Engineering Council. He also founded the Belgium-American Education Foundation, continuing support for children, the world's future.

Hoover worked with Democrat President Woodrow Wilson on the Paris Peace Talks of 1919. Wilson wanted Hoover to be his successor, but Hoover favored the Republican Party. In 1921 he headed the Russian Famine Relief, against the advice of fellow Republicans. When Warren Harding asked him to become Secretary of Commerce in 1921, Hoover did not sit still in a Washington D.C. office. He became Chair of the Colorado River Commission developing the water contract dividing water between California and Arizona; and the Hoover Dam.

Many basic regulatory and complementary methods of modern American living were originated and developed through the creative leadership of this Quaker humanitarian. Here is a list of some of accepted developments he initiated.

*   The American Children's Fund;
*   The National Aviation Conference, developing universal airport standards;
*   The Better Homes for Americans Program, promoting home ownership bank loans;
*   The American Child Health Association, to furnish every child with health care;

* The Hoover Street and Highway Safety Commission, the forerunner to the National Safety Council, developing uniform auto and industry safety standards;
* The St. Lawrence Waterway Comm. and The Rio Grande River Comm. negotiating Treaties between nations for river usage and boundaries;
* The Mississippi Flood Relief, utilizing federal money and local citizens; and
* The First International Radio-Telegraph Conference, recognizing the value and need for uniformity in communication standards worldwide.

Better known in the USA than Presidents Harding and Coolidge, Americans elected Hoover President of the United States in 1928.

Still giddy with the post-war era prosperity, Americans rich and poor ignored the worldwide depression rearing its head. Europe had no money to buy the shiploads of American food nor could they repay war loans. US farmers grew world-sized crops for one nation glutting the market, forcing prices down; manufacturers made the same mistake. Meanwhile innovative industrialists like Henry Ford reduced workers through utilizing manufacturing assembly lines.

The U.S. stock market balloon was ready to burst. Wall Street managers hid the truth from everyone, including President Hoover. During the WWI and for several years the stock market thrived; millions investing and selling shares for profit. Hoover requested Wall Street reports. He had been in the White House eight months, when he received a report from J.P. Morgan's spokesman, Thomas Lamont on **Oct. 19, 1929**. "The millennium has not only arrived but could continue through out your presidency- **if** and in Lamont's view, only **if**, Hoover followed the lead of his predecessor and agreed 'not to rock the boat."[23]

"At 11:30 A.M. Thursday, Oct. 24th a wave of liquidation swept the New York Stock Exchange."

The truth was 4,000 banks had failed and the stock market had been swinging up and down like a yoyo. When a stock price fell,

---

[23] *&³ The Day The Bubble Burst by Gordon Thomas & Max Morgan-Witt*

key players rushed in and bought shares to boost it up. They propped up stocks until they could no longer rob Peter to pay Paul. Foreign investors played the game as well.

Turbulent America was morphing from an agrarian nation to a leader in manufacturing and services. Hoover determined the USA would remain on the gold standard. However, non-payment of war loans by debtor- nations compounded cash flow problems; the world wide recession was deeper than anyone had foreseen. Only little Finland repaid its WWI debts.

The public enjoyed the fabulous twenties, but quickly tired of the broken economy and high unemployment of the 1930's. The man who fed Europe did not communicate well with the hurting American citizens. The people needed assurances. By 1930, a Democratic House and Senate blocked Hoover's efforts to make changes. Hoover's innovative legislation like Head Start was lost in concerns for jobs, jobs, jobs.

"And next there was a huge tent, ragged, torn in strips and the tears mended with pieces of wire...There were forty tents and shacks, and beside each habitation some kind of automobile. Far down the line, a few children stood and stared at the newly arrived truck,

"Anybody own this place, that we got to see 'fore we can camp?"
"You wanta camp here?"
"You, Never been in Hooverville before?"
"Where's Hooverville?"
"This here's her." [24]

Hooverville shanty towns became the butt of jokes and Herbert Hoover became the designated villain of the Great Depression. Quaker Hoover did not discuss his beliefs nor express verbally his faith and compassion. Sadly, most Americans associate Hoover with the depression, not realizing that one man in eight months could not have created national or international economic collapse. Few of the Wall Street manipulators were jailed, but several committed suicide or went broke along with the nation itself. General Douglas MacArthur's ruthless attack on the WWI Bonus marchers seeking

---

[24] 3 *Grapes of Wrath* by John Steinbeck

payments in Washington DC, added to the peoples' bitterness. Hoover got the blame, not MacArthur.

Franklin D .Roosevelt elected in 1932, calmed the people at his Fireside Chats, though he too, was unable to slow or stop the depression. Both he and Hoover underestimated the depth of the American economic problems. Hoover believed the capitalistic system would right itself; Roosevelt believed strongly in government intervention. FDR's Brain Trust developed laws, but they also dusted off and passed many Hoover-originated pieces of legislation. The USA got back on its financial feet during WWII.

Hoover suffered in silence. The Quaker faith does not encourage angry responses, even to untruthful whispering campaigns in the halls of Congress, and bald faced lies in the press.

A workaholic, Hoover's one safety valve for relaxation was fishing. He reeled them in, both on the Shenandoah River in VA and the McKenzie River in OR. Longtime Oregon guide, Rube Montgomery, observed that he and Hoover fished all day, rarely exchanging a word.

Once out of office, Hoover quietly founded Boys Clubs of America, Finnish Relief Fund, Polish Relief Fund, The Committee on Food for Small Democracies, and President's Famine Emergency Committee.

Few realize Herbert Hoover founded UNICEF, and was co-founder of CARE, two major United Nations (UN) international humanitarian organizations. He founded the Hoover Institute at Stanford and wrote sixteen scholarly books.

President Truman called on Hoover to assist with the Marshall Plan and work on hunger problems. Hoover's creed was that race, beliefs or nation didn't matter: "Relief is for all." His WWI organizational plans remained the basis for the WWII Marshall Plan and are still utilized by successful Non-Governmental Organizations (NGO's) across the world who feed millions, give medical care, build schools, plant crops, drill water systems, and start self employment programs. Hoover believed in people's ability to work, create and achieve success.

Popularity polls in the USA ignore the man who kept millions alive by the greatest humanitarian aid since the Jews ate manna in the wilderness. However, Europeans honor Hoover to this day because he saved their parents and grandparents from starvation. The Herbert Hoover Presidential Library Museum in Iowa has over 400 WWI flour sacks embroidered and sent in gratitude to the "Great Humanitarian Engineer." Europe has plaques honoring Hoover who stopped building personal income. A godly man, he dedicated his skills to serve peoples' needs. From 1914 until his death, Hoover the mining engineer, dedicated his life to public service for not just his nation, but a hurting world.

He believed in American capitalism and the spirit and willingness of Americans to initiate humanitarian services. The USA's depression-tested, greed-weakened capitalism survived the socialists- Marxists attempt to replace it. Dismantling capitalism remains a looming threat today, in spite of the fact that it has lifted many nations up so that 80% of the world lives better than they did in 1950.

Herbert Hoover died in 1964, a great leader and humanitarian, one of the most undervalued heroes and statesmen of America.

When blamed for not solving the Great Depression's ills, Hoover dedicated his life to proving the American system of constitutional and economic values, benefits all segments of society, especially the children. His actions, not his words, developed essential programs for every citizen's health, education and safety, in this greatest of nations. He loved America, the land of opportunity, where an orphan boy can have an education, prosper and even grow up to become president.

Hoover-Minthorne House Museum, 115 S River St, Newberg, OR 97132

Herbert Hoover Presidential Library, P. O. Box 468, West Branch, Iowa 52358

GOD'S UNDERCOVER AGENT

"I will pour out my spirit on all flesh; your sons and your daughters shall prophesy, your old men shall dream dreams, and your young men shall see visions"   *Joel 3: 28 NRSV*

*L*ittle Andrew slipped quietly out of bed, sneaking past his parent's bedroom to the kitchen. He filled a box with sugar, noting not much was left in the big jar. Out the squeaky back door into the darkness he ran towards the Witte police station. It was now home to the German troops who invaded The Netherlands several months ago. He crept up to the trucks, carefully looking around. Seeing no one, he loosened the gas cap on truck one and truck two, pouring the precious sugar into the tanks. Andrew made sure he was not being watched; then dashed back to his warm bed. When the German trucks couldn't move and the soldiers swore, Andrew smiled, knowing that sugar in the gas tanks was effective. He also lit firecrackers startling the German soldiers. Andrew loved the intrigue and action! If his parents knew what he was doing not a word was said, except 'how fast the sugar seemed to disappear these days.'

His mother was not surprised years later when Andrew joined the Army to help the futile, Dutch battle to retain Indonesia. An enemy shot in his foot disabled him.

Back in Witte, angry with his hospital stay and impaired body, he smoked and drank in excess. His dreams of daring wars, spying and intrigue were now ended. Yet, he needed something more. Little did he know what God had in store for him!

Before his frail, little mother's death, she brought her Bible to him and asked him to read it. One day Andrew reached for the Bible and after much reading and study, he said a simple prayer, "Lord, if You will show me the way, I will follow You. Amen."

Andrew worked for a couple of years before attending London's Worldwide Evangelism Crusade School (WEC). His foot improved gradually, though he still limped and suffered extreme back pains. He was often so short of money he barely had food and basic necessities.

Andrew returned to the Netherlands following his WEC schooling. He felt led to attend a 1955 Communist Youth Festival in Warsaw, Poland. He brought a few clothes and a few Bibles in his suitcase to Warsaw even though he didn't know the language. He managed to use gestures to a taxi driver who took him to a Baptist church where he found a lady who could speak German to translate for him. Andrew preached his first sermon behind the Iron Curtain through this older woman.

That afternoon thousands of Polish youth marched in the streets full of enthusiasm "For the taking off of old shackles and superstitions of religion and God. Man is his own master: the future is his to take."

Brother Andrew sat on bench watching the marchers' enthusiasm, with a Bible in his lap, pages ruffling in the breeze. He put his hand to hold them still and found himself looking at the book of Revelation, fingers resting on the verses..."Awake, and strengthen what remains and is on the point of death..." Through a blur of tears, he suddenly realized these words were guiding him to work behind the Iron Curtain, where the remnant Church was struggling for its life. But what could one man do compared to the thousands being swept up into Communism?

Returning to Amsterdam Andrew visited Christian friends who had befriended the limping, confused, but inspired young Christian. They encouraged him to lean on the Holy Spirit's strength, not his own. They also believed and confirmed through prayer, that his vision in Warsaw was from God.

When he spoke at their church, letting people know life was harsh for Christians living behind the Iron Curtain, he was selected for a team going to Czechoslovakia for four weeks. Upon arrival the guide told the team, "It's unpatriotic to be a Christian here; Church members are blackballed at work; can't attend school." He gave Andrew a pin in the shape of tiny cup which Christians called "the Cup of Suffering."

The Amsterdam Christians gave Andrew a Volkswagen bug which became his home. With it His lifelong ministry was launched, called Open Doors. The little car was his instrument for delivering Bibles and hope to the Christians who felt deserted and alone in Eastern Europe. For years he worked alone, but gradually added supporting partners and working teams. He wrote articles for newspapers that brought donations from Dutch Christians who wanted to help their fellow Europeans. Between Bible deliveries, he courted and married his beloved Corrie, who patiently shared his visions.

Andrew, the risk taker, was still a novice at depending on the Holy Spirit rather than his own ideas. "Occasional miracles and emergency dispensations get you out of difficult spots, but Andrew you need to learn to lean back in the arms of a Father who has more than enough to spare," taught his Amsterdam mentors.

Miracles occurred time after time as he traveled to nations behind the Iron Curtain in his Bible-packed 'bug.' Andrew was humbled to find how much his encouragement meant to believers who were scorned, isolated, and unable to meet or worship openly. Every check point was nerve racking, but somehow when the guards stopped him there would be a distraction and he would be allowed to enter Eastern Bloc nations without a full search of the car. Guard's eyes were blind to what type of books filled the back seat, the trunk, fenders and any space not needed for the motor. There were many close calls when Andrew should have been jailed or killed. Miraculous interventions occurred frequently. Directions out of the blue would advise him to avoid the main street and escape down back alleys. His dream of undercover adventures was realized smuggling Bibles and love, rather than guns and hate behind the Iron Curtain. The little boy who fought back against the German occupiers, still spends his time spreading Kingdom Love in all the world. Open Doors, one of the worlds' largest prayer teams and support organizations, goes where others do not or cannot. They place local language Bibles within nations where Bibles are forbidden, and reinforce oppressed Christians.

While many governments destroy homes and churches, arrest, torture and imprison Christians, faith grows stronger and numbers of new believers increase. Assisted by Open Doors and other loving groups, clerical supplies, food, Bibles and survival income, via God's loving peaceful espionage, appear consistently in the darkest places. Open Doors knows practicing nonviolent Kingdom Love is thrilling as well as beneficial to the human race!

Wife Corrie, Andrews's brothers and sisters, and many Christians in The Netherlands prayed, collected Bibles, coats, warm blankets and money for his early missions. As word spread, Christians from around the world joined with prayers and donations. During the cold war thousands of Bibles were delivered to countries in their languages, even Russia. Brother Andrew, the small, blue-eyed Dutch man blended into the Eastern bloc nations as he preached and encouraged people who were spiritually hungry, lonely and mistreated due to their Christian faith.

One day when the VW bug's speedometer showed 225,000 miles, it broke down in West Germany. It needed a new motor and the garage needed 500 marks to repair it. Andrew told them to go ahead, but when he exchanged his money for marks he only had 470. Just as he reached the garage to pick up the car his team members ran, yelling at him, "Andrew, this lady just asked us if we were the Dutchmen and when we said 'yes,' she gave us 50 marks." Round the clock prayers by Corrie and thousands of supporters backed Open Doors' Bible delivery trips and Holy Spirit rescues. Every trip was life threatening.

The teams developed a policy at Guard Stations when there were two or three in the van, only one would talk to the guards while the others remained in constant prayer until they had passed inspection and were on their way.

Eventually, Andrew visited Russia itself and delivered Bibles. As late as 1964 Bibles were still not welcomed, but the people were in deep need of them, especially the Pastors.

Open Doors began making Russian deliveries in a van, using special words and meeting places with local Christians. When the shooting war was over Andrew served on a Culture Committee and in the process promised the Russian Orthodox Church leaders a million Bibles that Open Doors was able to deliver as a gift from the western Christians to their eastern Christian brothers.

The Open Doors team grew to twelve through whom thousands of Bibles flowed regularly into Eastern Europe and Russia. Eastern Bloc Christians were 'strengthened from the point of death.' knowing they were not forgotten by their fellow Western Christians. The KGB tracked The International Open Doors Organization, documenting 142 pages of team visits smuggling Bibles and love behind the Iron Curtain.

Open Doors' Eastern bloc Bible smuggling was Act One of a remarkable ministry. Brother Andrew's 1965 visit to China tore at his heart. Visiting a commune he asked to see their church and was told "You will find no churches. You see, religion is for the helpless. Here in China we are not helpless any more." He could find no Christians anywhere. A few Bibles and Bible stores existed in some cities, but could sell no product to anyone. He realized he must get Bibles to the Christians in this harsh land. Brother Andrew perceived that God needed dedicated, impassioned, visionary Chinese leaders, not Westerners, to achieve success behind the Bamboo Curtain.

Home once again in The Netherlands, Brother Andrew, Corrie and the team prayed that somehow the Holy Spirit would raise Chinese Christians who could share their dream and program to deliver Bibles to China.

MISSION STATEMENT FOR OPEN DOORS INTERNATIONAL

Open Doors' mission statement is based on I Corinthians 12:26: *"If one member suffers, all suffer together with it; if one member is honored, all rejoice together with it."*

"To strengthen and equip the Body of Christ living under or facing restriction and persecution because of their faith in Jesus Christ, and to encourage their involvement in world evangelism by:

- Providing Bibles and literature, media, leadership training, socio-economic development and through intercessory prayer;
- Preparing the Body of Christ living in threatened or unstable areas to face persecution and suffering; and
- Educating and mobilizing the Body of Christ living in the free world to identify with threatened and persecuted Christians and be actively involved in assisting them."

All material is based on "God's Smuggler" by Brother Andrew and John and Elizabeth Sherrill 1967 Signet Books

Open Doors Vision Statement www.opendoors.org

Joel 3:28 NRSV Bible

I Corinthians 12:26 NRSV Bible

OPEN HEARTS AT WORK

"...there are no closed doors to the Gospel and the Word of God is not in chains." (25)

Sponsors warned Fred and Edna Smith to expect luggage and personal body searches at the Moscow Airport. They made it through customs when one agent motioned to Fred, he needed a strip search. They both trembled, but tried to look calm.

"Well, I'll hold your coat and tie, go get it over with so we don't miss our tour," Edna said matter-of-factly. She tried to appear normal and relaxed while Fred followed the stern uniformed guard.

Finding Fred had nothing to confiscate the Smiths were free to climb onto the tour bus. After Fred placed their luggage in the rack he turned to hug Edna. Only then did Fred put on his coat, touching it gently, thrilled by feeling the small New Testaments which lined it from to top to bottom.

At the appointed house church Fred and Edna carefully opened the seams to reveal the cherished Bibles. The Russian Christians' love eased Fred's anxiety. Elated, the Smiths' hearts warmed as the Russians, some of whom spoke English, shared their testimonies. Natasha lives in a tiny apartment and spends most of her days seated on quilts, under a table where she types verses from a few torn Bible pages for others. The quilts deaden the sound of typing so that no one living in apartments above, below and on either side would know. Betrayal of Christians by ardent Communists was resulting in imprisonment or the Gulag from which many never return. Natasha caressed the little New Testament the Smith's gave her. Now she can type more pages for believers.

The Smiths' last Bible was given to a woman and her son who had walked for three days when they heard Bibles might be coming. Wearing shabby clothes, tired and hungry, the older woman fell on her knees kissing the Bible and praying, while tears of joy rolled down her cheeks.

Back home, the Smiths were guest speakers at our church singles' group, sharing their Russian adventures and inviting our congregation to attend next week's Open Doors' banquet where a member from an underground church would share what life is like for Christians living under religious oppression.

Fred challenged us. "You Americans can attend church or not, read a Bible and pray anytime or place you wish. Open Doors International recognizes the need to challenge hearts of free Christians to sympathetic support for persecuted sisters and brothers. They need your prayers and material help if they are to survive."

At the banquet a young Filipino House Boy described his nightmare years in a Saudi Arabian prison after he and some of his fellow workers' apartments were raided during an informal Communion Service. Each was imprisoned for several years. He continued speaking quietly to the prison guards about Jesus Christ. Beatings and torture crippled this man, who on his release date was re-sentenced for another two years, for the crime of not renouncing his Christian faith. His face glowed as he testified that the Lord remained faithful. He had been able to have a positive influence with prisoners and guards as well as the children in the Saudi household where he had been employed. Now he could return home to his family in Manila.

Local businessmen and women underwrite Annual Open Doors banquets across America, for Christian victim awareness and to raise vital funds. Like Billy Graham, Brother Andrew and his family receive a modest salary as do Open Door employees. Brother Andrew and his wife Corrie share their home with staff; store clothes and blankets; and even mortgage it when funds for Bibles are lacking.

China's and Russia's governments are known for their Communist Manifestos that tossed God out and replaced Him with the "State" as the people's savior. Unfortunately in parts of the Middle East, there is zero-tolerance for Christians, Jews and especially anyone who converts from Islam, where Sharia Law is practiced.

But the Christians in those lands have not replaced Jesus their Lord with the "State" or Muhammad. Worldwide Christians churches and organizations like Open Doors are assisting their suffering sisters and brothers. Open Doors' monthly newsletter alerts supporters and prayer teams to victories as well as mistreatment across the world. Many Christians were surprised by increased persecution of Jews and Christians in Middle East nations where Jews were present 2,000 earlier than Jesus' ministry in the first century and five hundred and seventy years before Mohammed was born.

Due to conflicts of religion and lifestyles Christian missionaries establish fewer clinics, schools and churches in Islamic nations. Antagonistic, ambitious leaders still utilize hatred of the Crusades to foment anger against "The Infidels." In actuality, Crusaders killed as many or more Jews, as they did Arabs in the short-lived six Crusades. During a 200-year period there were six Crusades, none of which lasted longer than three years. Their purpose was to allow Christians to visit and enjoy the land of Jesus and the Jews. The Arabs retained control over most of the area. In Israel today there are thousands of Arab Muslims living peacefully, serving in the government, schools and businesses with their Jewish counterparts. Likewise Arab Christians live there as well.

Brother Andrew quoted Abraham's prayer from Genesis 17:18 *"If only Ishmael might live under your blessing!"* when he launched a ten-year prayer campaign for the Muslims. He explained, "As long as we have an enemy image of a group of people we cannot love them. We must remember that Christ died for Muslims as He died for every one of us. We need to stand up, listen to God's calling and be his church."

Open Doors supplies Bibles in Farsi, Aramaic and Arabic languages as well as opening small businesses with local citizens in many Muslim countries. Affected adversely by the Wahhabism[25] version of Islam, Christian and Jewish minorities who have lived side by side with Muslims for centuries are no longer safe. The adoption

---

[25] Shari'a Law was begun in 1800 by Abd al Wahhab in Egypt

of Shari'a Law in several Muslim nations fosters increased mistreatment and death of Christian and Jewish believers. Daughters and sons are brain washed in schools and mosques to hate the infidels. People are arrested for owning a Bible; many are imprisoned for years; and/ or beaten unmercifully by gangs while the governments turns a blind eye. Sadly, in Iran, following the release of abused leaders from jail, they are often killed by unexplained circumstances. One former Islamist said that in his country the price of serving Jesus is not "if I am killed, but *when* I am killed.

American Open Doors Banquets culminate in the annual International Meeting held in Costa Mesa, California. Attendees may take no pictures; names used by the speakers are changed to protect them. These gentle people, both men and women from anti-Christian areas, share their miraculous victories, as well as abuses. They lovingly tell how they were healed from diseases and demons; how miraculous deliveries of food arrived when they were starving; and of financial and spiritual evidence of the Lord's love for them. Though many are shunned and isolated from their families and fellow countrymen, their eyes are aglow with love. Tears of joy flow as attendees and speakers' spirits are uplifted. The Holy Spirit enriches and empowers the conference during a twenty-four hour prayer vigil following the Day of Sharing.

A recently widowed minister's wife from Cuba, in her early twenties was barely able to talk. Her husband held house church meetings. She was very tender from his recent death at the hands of the police. They arrested him, tortured him, cut off his head and displayed it on a post after throwing his body on her porch. Christians' bravery from many nations most Americans can't even locate on a map, is humbling.

Among these faithful believers in Costa Mesa, was a casually dressed middle aged man, small with blond hair and intense blue eyes. It was Brother Andrew himself. He was unassuming and natural, until he addressed the crowd at the evening meal. Filled with love and first hand knowledge, he challenges Christians to stretch further for the Kingdom. Radiating like a laser beam Brother Andrew, unleashed love, compassion and real world challenges into attendees' minds and hearts.

Someone asked if Corrie was here. He answered. "We find that it is no longer safe for us to travel together. She is home. It seems that in many nations our blond coloring makes us targets for death hits. Since I was a young man, I have lived with death, a bad back and the call to bring the word of God's love to the world. I do not want to endanger or place Corrie in jeopardy."

Sad and happy tears flow frequently during meetings laced with believer's stories of abuse, imprisonment, and loss of jobs and homes, but always offset by great joy, miracles, and Jesus' love. Victorious spiritual living in nations rabid in their desire to destroy Christianity and Judaism, cuts into American's comfortable complacency.

"The determining factor for Open Doors involvement anywhere in the world is the presence of a Persecuted Church. We stand alongside when the Body of Christ has run into problems because of its own identity. We have voluntarily limited ourselves to the needs of the Persecuted church – in the Body of Christ. We go where others do not go, and do what others do not do. Ours is not a competitive vision. If others are doing the job, we leave it to them. We want to concentrate our limited resources on the neediest part of the world," said Brother Andrew in his closing.

The entire week-end was filled with the blessings and presence of the Holy Spirit. The sharing and prayer made hearts more tender and caring for fellow Christians. Encouraged by Brother Andrew's vision and faith, thousands of Christians like Fred and Edna Smith, will risk their lives to carry Bibles and Christian supplies to oppressed Christian brothers and sisters across the world. Others gladly donate regular monthly support and millions pray fervently. Open Doors Members also believe in the verse that prompted Brother Andrew to begin smuggling Bibles into Russia. "Wake up and strengthen what remains and is on the point of death."

---

(25) "God's Smuggler" by Brother Andrew
Smith testimony in Scottsdale United Methodist Church 1984
Open Doors Meeting, Costa Mesa, CA 1985

OPERATION PEARL
TO CHINA WITH LOVE

$\mathcal{L}$ined up like they were vermin by the Chinese troops, the frightened men, women and children shuddered; some cried and clung to one another.

"These people have sinned against the State." The officer's angry voice rang out over the large crowd. "Now they will pay the price."

As guards released the safety catches on their rifles Mrs. Kwang, one of the victims, silently prayed, "Father forgive them," "Take aim. Fire! The crack of rifle shots echoed through the square as bullets flew into the men and women lined up before them. Many instantly slumped to the ground, while others remained standing. Among those unhurt was Mrs. Kwang. She hurriedly slipped into the mob of viewers and snuck home.

When Mao defeated Chaing Kei-shek in 1949, he also killed thirty million Christians. Under the new rules, no religion can exist in China except Communism, the new Chinese Religion. Following frequent massacres by firing squads, many believers became fearful, losing their faith. The persecuted church in China began to discover who the Real Believers were.

Far away in Los Angeles Billy Graham was holding a Christian Crusade which lasted for many weeks. One of the attendees was an ex-Marine, handsome, strong, self- assured and not particularly interested in church. Because it pleased his wife, he came to the crusade again the second evening, He felt pulled from the top of the stadium down the steps forward to the platform with thousands of others as unshed tears from the past came pouring forth.

Graham continued," God is spirit and those who worship Him must worship Him in spirit and truth. God is speaking to someone tonight in his late twenties – which he must humble himself and be converted, like a child he should believe."

A spiritual force moved David changing his life forever. David, the young ex-Marine and his wife Julie had the strong urge to be in mission for God following the crusade where Billy said, "Many of you have heard about Jesus all your life. What I want to ask you tonight is have you ever met Jesus personally?"

Operation Pearl

Though it was unthinkable in the minds of most, prayers by Chinese Christians were answered in the time of their darkest period of pain, suffering and isolation. Operation Pearl was developed step by careful step; birthed by millions of praying Christians around the world, spiritual visions and donations of ordinary people. They heard and responded to God's love song for his Asian children. Kingdom love is capable of so much with the Holy Spirit's leading.

Although he did not know it, David's destiny was tied to the execution survivor, Mrs. Kwang, Brother Andrew and Operation Pearl, the world's largest Bible delivery into a nation completely closed to Christianity.

Bible studies kept pointing David, a printer by trade, to things like Mark 13:10: "And the Gospel must be published in all nations" and Psalm 68:11: "The Lord gave the word; great was the company of those that published it."[26] He caught on that somehow he was to publish the gospel, but where and when? It all fell into place when he was hired by The Far East Broadcast Company (FEBC) to go to the Philippines. He did assorted things like printing, youth development and work with local hardship situations. Sometimes they had little to eat, but somehow food would arrive or an unexpected check. David

---

[26] King James Version

and wife, Julie learned to trust, even when the pantry was empty and a child was ill.

A mutual worker began talking about the need for Bibles in China. David was amazed that anyone would consider it. When Mao forced Chaing Kei-shek and his followers to Taiwan he ran off all foreign missionaries and preachers (Included in those ejected were Bob Pierce, WV and Harry Haines, UMCOR). That first year Mao permitted Christians to worship and then new laws ruled that no religion could exist except Communism, the Chinese Religion.

Systematically families of all educated people were broken up with the children sent to work farms where they were brainwashed with communism; the parents were separated and put to work far away in factories or on farms. Because Communism cannot exist along side Christianity dictators expunged Christianity from society. The new laws permitted only one child per family and all others to be aborted. Heavy fines, torture, imprisonment and death made the laws effective immediately. Most families preferred to keep their boy babies, creating a population within China of millions of young men with too few females available for dating or marriage.

Bibles were replaced by Mao's pocket- sized Little Red Book so everyone knew the new Chinese laws. The official Chinese Language for the entire mainland became Mandarin; only in Hong Kong and Canton was Cantonese permitted. After Mao's death the Three Self Churches were permitted: Self Government, Self Support and Self Propagated.[27] All attendees are registered; government spies attend worship to report if government and its laws are negated. Three Self members meet in the old churches; those not confiscated for factories, offices or were torn down. No church can be repaired nor new ones built. The New Christian Manifesto states that everyone pledges to support the People's Government and Communism. All Bibles were burned; prison was the consequence of anyone withholding a Bible or hiding one.

Brother Andrew prayed and tried to make contact with Chinese believers, but a Bamboo Wall sealed the natives in and foreigners

---

[27] The Government permits registered Three Self churches which follow the rules and do not fight Communism.

out. Meanwhile, as David did his work, he kept getting promptings about the Chinese Christians and their desperate need for Bibles. His fellow FEBC workers actually circulated a Newsletter which said, "China will open soon, are you ready?"

A little money became available allowing David to travel to Myanmar (Burma) where he met with some Christians who knew obscure mountain-routes into eastern China. His meeting with some Wycliffe translators gave him hope about ways to get some Bibles inside China.

Bro. Andrew and Corrie Ten Boom, Dutch survivor of the Holocaust, were traveling in Burma also and met with the same Wycliffe translators who mentioned David's visit. Bro. Andrew sent a letter to David inviting him to The Netherlands. But David had no money for such trips. He just prayed that these promptings and urgings from God would give him direction.

FEBC needed David in America for several months, sending him to Chicago to a large meeting where he represented FEBC. When he spoke of China to some of the various leaders they replied, "China is closed and you are talking about Bibles into China? No way. We have to work where we are permitted to go."

A New York City friend invited David and paid the airfare to New York. There David was blessed with another gift from a former FEBC employee, whom God had instructed to save money for David, even though they were not working together any longer. The envelope contained $300, enough to fly to The Netherlands.

At Brother Andrew's home, the men talked and David observed this small man with his children in the garden working and laughing. He seemed like any other father until he was in his study, praying on his knees for China.

Miracles continued. Both Brother Andrew and David realized that the new Bibles needed to be the same size a Mao's Red Book so that no one could tell what was being carried in a shirt pocket or purse. When Bro. Andrew was in Burma and China, he left Bibles lying around. People just left them or found him and returned them as 'they don't need Bibles any more since Communism.' Bro. Andrew and Open Doors ordered 25,000 Mandarin Chinese Bibles and hired

David as part of their team. Their motto was "Seek and Save" as opposed to "Search and Destroy."

Back in the Philippines the Bibles were printed, packed and taken for distribution by the people David had located earlier. Mountain traders carried Bibles by donkey over steep passes into China, a few at a time over a period of several months, until twenty-five thousand were in Chinese hands.

Within China during the 1970's, Christians suffered harsh repressions; mob trials; and physical torture. Hong Kong Chinese with whom David had began meeting, had families in China, but were reluctant to place them in harm's way delivering Bibles.

A few people tried carrying Bibles into China, like Pastor Ling. He was forced to flee to Laos after torture and his right arm was cut off. Hearing via the grapevine that Bibles for China were coming, Ling walked 20 days to meet with David in Hong Kong. Among other Christians was Sister Woo, a frail, elderly lady, Joseph and his Uncle Liu. She invited the men to tea at her home.

Sister Woo told of her dream of a map and an address where a woman greeted two Hong Kong Chinese men who wanted to deliver Bibles someday. This seemed to affirm their vision. Through faith and a lot of prayer they had the confidence to believe Bible deliveries inside China was God's will. From these meetings were developed contacts in some provinces of China where revival meetings and healings were occurring and Christian house churches were growing. David likened the network of Chinese Christians to the veins in a leaf which feed the rest of the leaf. Strengthened by the prayers of a worldwide prayer team, these Chinese Christians developed major networks for a future dream,the delivery of one million Bibles into China.

Contacts by outsiders brought courage to the Chinese Christians who realized they were not alone. The few Bibles they had were worn out or had been torn into pages to be passed around and shared. Christians being saved in house church revivals needed the word of God! One of the key persons who developed these delicate networks was Mrs. Kwang, who survived unscathed from her firing squad experience. However, she suffered the loss of her husband and son to the police brutality. She spent time in prison and was tortured, but was encouraged by visions and miraculous interventions by the Holy Spirit. As she kept on preaching, teaching, and revivals occurred where ever she went. In prayer she would regularly receive messages to leave or to hide. Her faith increased along with her effectiveness in sharing Christ's love for the Chinese people.

The development of Operation Pearl involved the international prayer teams, and perfect planning. Supported by the donations of many loving Christians, specific people worked over three years, finding the crew and right barge to carry one million water-tight packaged Bibles. When the Chinese network felt they had been betrayed, the plan was stopped. It was reinstated three months later. Bible Day, June 18, 1981, a typhoon was reported and the crew prayed for two hours. The storm went away or played out, so they proceeded. In Hong Kong, Mrs. Kwang phoned mainland Chinese Christians to say that 'the patient was ready to be moved to the hospital if they were ready to receive.' Her responses were 'we are ready to receive.' David relayed this to Bro. Andrew who alerted prayer teams around the world that the Chinese courier team is in danger. "Pray for 72 hours."

The barge crew prayed to have clean hands and hearts. When they pulled anchor they knew they were covered in prayer. They indicated to the appropriate parties that 'we are having a party with eighteen bowls of rice and twenty-three cups of tea' meaning June 18, @ 2300 hours. One Chinese patrol boat with machine guns neared the barge, moving along side. The barge captain did not even look at its crew, moving on ahead while his team below prayed hard. No other boats were in sight when they reached the rendezvous beach, lowered, then tipped the deck, unloading the "Z" boats hauling strings of Bible packages. From behind the trees people popped out and loaded packages onto the shoulder poles and baskets, heading off into the dark. A few small trucks hauled some of the packages, but most went person by person on bicycles. In two hours the barge was unloaded and 11,100 packages of Bibles were on their way.

Prayers covered the entire two-hour operation: 1) floating the million Bibles wrapped in waterproof packages of ninety; 2) the specific barge designed for quick unloading; 3) the necessary knowledge of the waters and rules for Chinese shipping; 4) the correct Captain; and

5) the thousands of people with bicycles who picked up packages in the dead of night with barely a hitch.

When the police arrived there were only a few parcels floating in the water which were confiscated. Not a bicycle was observed. The police invaded homes of suspected Christians and searched for stored books. A few were found, but 99.9 percent were spread throughout China to feed the spiritual souls of the Christians. Later reports indicate that one person betrayed a few names to the police. A few leaders were tortured and imprisoned; however, nearly one million Bibles were distributed throughout China.

Bro. Andrew lamented that this was less than 1% of the needed Bibles. Continually, visitors smuggle Bibles into China and The Chinese Government now permits printing limited numbers of Bibles for the Three Self churches.

Ten years later on my visit to China our American guide wanted to visit a church service. It was held in an old building with a few older people in attendance. When we arrived the church ladies made tea. They very proudly showed us their new Bibles and hymnals. In the old, but very clean sanctuary, we listened to them preach and sing in Chinese and then sang "Amazing Grace" in English for them. After more tea while sitting on little plastic chairs, we quietly gifted a collection for them. One Chinese lady took my hand and held it against her check tenderly to express how much they appreciated the support of other Christians. In humility we left, full of admiration for their faith and keenly aware of the high price they pay for blessings we take for granted.

Open Doors continues to support Chinese Christians through prayers, Bibles and monetary gifts. When Christians are imprisoned, Open Doors shares names with the world prayer team. Though anyone arrested suffers abuse, isolation and torture; many are miraculously set free;

The murderous tyranny of Mao has ended along with the Gang of Four. The thirty plus million Chinese, mostly Christians, killed by Mao, is the largest slaughter of believers in history. After sixty years of Communist tyranny, a form of capitalism is broadening the economy for many Chinese; however, it is still dangerous to openly display Christian attitudes. Brother Andrew and the Open

Doors Teams continue to share God's love with Chinese who are far from free. The Bamboo Curtain seems to less solid, yet is far from being open.

For his part in the Bible delivery, Pastor Chen was arrested; He would not reveal any information about who, what, why or when. As the operation had taken place near Swatow police flew in investigators from Beijing. They placed Pastor Chen outside on top of a four foot box with a noose around his neck, standing without food or water. He tried to talk to his captors about Jesus, but they told him to be quiet. He prayed, he sang and he stood for 12 days, reminded of how Jesus must have looked from the cross at the men gambling for his clothes. The guards were amazed each day that he was there standing, not falling and hanging himself. On day thirteen a thunder and lightning storm hit the area. The lightning miraculously cut the rope but did not harm Pastor Chen, who fell to the ground. His captors held him and gave him water. They cried out, "Please don't die! We need to know about this Jesus. No one can stand for all these days and not die unless there is a miracle." With some food, water and rest, Pastor Chen was able to eventually return home, but not until he had led the interrogators in the sinners' prayer. He told them of God's love for all his children who repent and accept Jesus Christ. All the guards accepted Jesus Christ as their savior that day.

---

1) Bible references are from the King James Bible
2) "God's Smuggler to China" by Brother Andrew with Dan Wooding and Sara Bruce: Hodder and Stoughton 1981
3) "Unsolved Miracles" Compiled by John Van Diest; article by Jeff Tayler, Compass Direct, for Open Doors,.
4) "The Night of Miracles" by Paul Estabrooks

WE MUST LOVE WHOM?

"If only Ishmael might live under your blessing!"
(Genesis 17:18) NIV

Brother Andrew once stunned the emcee during a Christian TV interview when he said, "The Muslims are not our enemies."

"Well, if these people aren't our enemies, then who is?" "The Devil," Brother Andrew answered, "But never the people! As long as we have an enemy image of any group of people, we cannot love them. God does not call us to any nation or people for whom we do not shed tears when we pray for them. We are tempted to label them 'good guys' and 'bad guys', but the Middle East is far more complex than it appears. We need to go to all sides with the love of Jesus. In fact, we need to be like the angel Joshua met on the road to Jericho. He asked, 'Are you for us or for our enemies'? The angel replied, 'Neither'."

Brother Andrew's messages since the 1970's are filled with concern for the Middle East. The Open Doors prayer warriors set a 'ten-year prayer program' for the Middle East and all Islamic Nations. Prayer worked well for Russia and China, why not Islam?

"When are you going to visit the churches in Iran?" An Iranian pastor attending the 1978 Open Doors' Conference asked Brother Andrew and fellow employee, Johan. They were amazed. Iran's Ayatollah Khomeini was in power with a fanatical Islamic regime that condemned virtually anything seen as Western. Birthed in Israel,

Christianity is not a Western religion though the Muslim rulers indict it as 'western.'

It was 1981 before he was able to reach Iran and make his way to a small Christian church sitting next door to a huge mosque. Five times daily the calls to prayer brought hundreds of Muslims to the mosque, causing Brother Andrew to ask his team, "Are we Christians as willing to stand up for our faith as they are for theirs?"

He was pleasantly surprised that the church bookstore had copies of his book "God's Smuggler" in the Farsi language. Amazingly the Christians were not complaining about the economic, political and spiritual problems the Ayatollah had brought.

"God has been good to us," they said. Because of all the chaos and confusion, the church had been able to use the same permit five times to print more Bibles. More Muslims have been coming to the church and we Christians can share God's love with them, though we are not allowed to proselytize.

But his biggest surprise was their statement about Khomeini exposing Islam for what it really is; "he unwrapped Islam and showed the world what is really inside."

These Iranian Christians experienced Islam's darker side in the form of intolerance, harassment and frequent police surveillance and interrogation. Brother Andrew realized that no matter the circumstances, no country is closed to God's eyes! One Muslim Christian pastor whom Brother Andrew met, bade farewell saying, "Andrew, when, not if they kill me, it will be for speaking, not for being silent... When, not if."

Westerners forget that Arabs were a part of Pentecost. The Christian church existed in the Middle East nearly six hundred before Mohammad. Since the Crusades, Christian influence was weakened by Arab conquests and birthrates. Radical Shari'a Law in several nations inflames conflicts between Jews, Christians and Muslims.

The problems Christians face while living in Islamic nations are several pronged:

1) Radical Islamists attack innocent people; bomb buildings, shops, churches, markets and schools. They plan to rule everyone with no regrets for killing other Muslims along with infidels, the Christians and Jews;

2) Radical Islamists say all non-Islamic persons are our enemies; and
3) Radical Islamists rant about killing all the 'pigs' from Israel and 'great Satan', America.

The few valid reasons Muslims hate Westerners include resentment of the Crusade partial conquests that ended in 1248 and open envy of western advances while they remain in a sixth century mind set. But, rightfully, add to that our exporting decadence such as pornography, alcohol and drug usage they fear will influence their people negatively. However, there is much hypocrisy by more affluent Muslims who drink, womanize, gamble and do whatever they wish, while tightly controlling the less fortunate. Religious brainwashing that all people must accept Islam by force if necessary, lays beneath fearful actions by many Muslims. (One must wonder if this is the true message of the Quran.)

On his return to The Netherlands Brother Andrew was called by someone seeking a Christian pastor to pray for his father. The son was an aide to the late Chairman Arafat. Through this opportunity, a meeting with Brother Andrew and Yassir Arafat developed, that led to meetings with the leaders of Hamas and Hezbollah.

Background of Hatred of Israel 1948

The hatred between Jews and Palestinians was exacerbated prior to Israeli settlers' arrival to the United Nations (UN) establishment of Israel in May 1948. The Arab Defense League (ADL) distributed pamphlets throughout the region telling Palestinians to go visit relatives in Syria, Lebanon, Egypt and Iran before the Jews arrived to the UN land area designated to become the new Israel. They assured the Palestinians that ADL armies will kill the Jews before they even established themselves, then the Palestinians could return home safely. Thousands of Arab families traveled with suitcases, assured that after the Arab-planned war killed all the Jews, they could return home.

However, The Jews defeated the ADL armies which left these Palestinians stranded in nations that did not want them permanently.

For this reason many Palestinians became refugees. Gradually, many of them began coming back. They resented losing land to Jews.

Should they not also resent their fellow Arabs who lured them away only later to push them out? The thousands of Arabs, who remained home, live and work peacefully alongside their Jewish neighbors.

The Israelis have been forced to fight three wars with the ADL, wars that Israel won, adding more land to their holdings, including Jerusalem, which was not part of the original land designated by the UN in 1948. Voluntarily the Jews gave back portions of lands they won.

The West Bank, December 1992

Two armed attacks left six Israeli soldiers dead and one kidnapped. The Islamic Hamas claimed responsibility and wanted a prisoner exchange with release of Sheikh Ahmand Yassin, founder of Hamas. The body of the kidnapped Israeli soldier was found three days later. The Israelis conducted a lightening-quick retribution by picking up 400 leaders in Palestine. Israel hoped to cut off the head of Hamas. They removed these men to a remote mountain area camp, Marj al-Zohour. Agreements negotiated between the Israelis and the PLO proved to be worthless. PLO leadership did not respond to the local peoples' needs and their Arab brothers and sisters in nearby Arab nations offered no help. Many Palestinians felt abandoned and helpless. The resistance movement was fueled to such a degree that Hamas became a strong organization backed by hopeless people.

Lebanon: January 1993

Brother Andrew realized the leaders of the Hamas, needed to hear the gospel; to know that God loves everyone. In spite of people advising against it, January 1993, he slipped into Marj al-Zohour, the southernmost Lebanon mountainous region where the Palestinian leaders were being held by the Israelis.

He met with Dr. Abjulaziz Rantisi, the second in command of Hamas. It was wet, muddy and bitterly cold. A box of potatoes was their only food, but as Dr. Rantisi told him, every one of these tents is a mosque. The men seemed grateful for Brother Andrew's caring; they accepted Arabic Bibles and books. When the US government brokered a compromise with Israel regarding the return of these prisoners to Palestine in a year, the men in the camp knew international laws were being broken. They voted unanimously to reject the American-Israeli deal.

"God take revenge on those who suppressed us. God take our revenge on those who expelled us!" Thus Hamas' resentment of the Israelis became deep hatred.

Voorthuizen, The Netherlands, April 2002
The Musalaha Conference
(Musalaha is Arabic meaning 'forgiveness and reconciliation')

In 1988 in Bethlehem, Salim a part-time teacher at Bethlehem Bible College had a vision to bring Messianic Jews and Palestinian Followers of Christ (Both Christians but cultural enemies) together. The impetus for this meeting came from God to Salim in prayer. Perhaps we can be examples and models, showing that it is possible to live side by side, free from the bondage of hatred. He sensed God asking him, "Do you love My Children? Do you love My Arab children? How about My Palestinian children?" The Pastor began explaining to God, 'You know they are our enemies,' but was overcome with a feeling of shame.

Thus in April 2002, ninety-four Pastors, church leaders and families flew out of the war zone that was currently Israel and the West Bank, courtesy of Near East Ministry.

The Middle East situation was: *"Israeli army's incursions into the West Bank after a spate of suicide bombings left angry Palestinians. Tanks patrolled Bethlehem. Curfews were imposed on Hebron. Fierce resistance faced the Israeli army in the Jenin Lebanon refugee camp."*

That these pastors and families could get out was a miracle as it was virtually impossible for Palestinians and Jews to meet inside the country. Though both groups were Christians, the Palestinians sat on one side of the room and Jewish believers sat on the other. Brother Andrew was an invited guest.

Salim took a deep breath…"We are two nations living in one house. We share the living room, the kitchen, the corridor, the bathroom, the toilet, but not the bedroom. The fact is we do not like one another. Worse still, we hate one another."

"We need to evaluate our conflicts.

* The First Problem is the division between *us* and *them*. Each side blames the other, saying that they have lost all moral and ethical standards. We are able to understand our own group and recognize its good qualities while overlooking our shortcomings, because it is important to distinguish between *us* (who are right and good and merciful) and *them* (who are evil and wrong).

* The Second problem is our failure to see plurality within the other side. We generalize the stereotype of the other, saying things like, 'They all hate us and want to kill us'. We are unable to see them as individuals with unique feelings and thoughts. Due to the language barrier Israelis and Palestinians, do not read each other's newspapers. Thus each side is dependent on very selective information given about us by the other side.

* The Third problem is each thinking they are morally superior. Thus we decide that we are more peace loving, trustworthy, and honest; therefore, we view with contempt those who have different values.

* The Fourth Problem is the perception by each side that they are victims and thus they are unable to see themselves as a threat to the other. If we are victims, then we cannot be the victimizers. The victims' mentality causes us to be blind to the others' pain, aspirations and needs.

"However, this week," Salim continued, "We have a wonderful opportunity to break through these barriers and recognize that each person, whether Jew or Palestinian Christian, is created in the image of God and is redeemed by the blood of the Messiah. Paul instructs on how to treat one another: 'Be devoted to one another in brotherly love. Honor one another above yourselves…Bless those who persecute you; bless and do not curse…Do not repay anyone evil for evil… Do not take revenge, my friends, but leave room for God's wrath… Do not be overcome by evil, but overcome evil with good.'"

Together in Arabic, Hebrew and English they sang the theme song, written by Lisa Loden for the Musalaha:

> *"He is our peace, we shall be one. He is our reconciliation. The wall of partition He's broken down. He is our peace; we shall be one."*

The preaching from both sides acknowledged ..."I cannot love God and at the same time hate my brothers in Christ. Palestinians, just like Jews, are sons of Adam and Abraham...we are all so wounded... we need healing and rest."

"If you are offering your gift on the alter and remember that your brother has something against you, leave your gift go, be reconciled to your brother; then come offer your gift."

Brother Andrew spoke..."The wall that was built to keep people and nations apart has come down here in a mighty demonstration of the power of God. And as dedicated Christians, our reaction is: If God can do this to a few dozen people, He can do it to a million people...Oh that hearts may be gripped by the potential power of Jesus to bring people together: Israelis and Palestinians, Christians in the West and in the East, starting where we should have been all this time – at the foot of the cross. There is only one name given under heaven whereby we must be saved, and that includes saved from violence and terrorism, hatred and revenge. God has already taken the initiative and now calls all of us to follow. Yes, we've discovered the principle of God's solution. Now we must continue and work hard to see this Musalaha concept of God's forgiveness and love becomes a movement – like a mighty river, a flood not just a trickle!"

Brother Andrew realized God had led this wonderful agape love retreat, keeping him inspired and motivated.

In spite of the fact that many Christians are abused, imprisoned and martyred annually, 125,000 new Christian convert weekly, of whom 16,000 are Muslims. The fastest growth is found in Asia, the Middle East, Africa, Latin America, Eastern Europe and Indonesia. Radio and television dishes bring God's word in their varied languages from satellites covering the earth. Though thousands suffer damaged homes, churches and martyrdom, the Jesus dreams and visions, occur with great frequency. Healings of the sick are common; demons are being expelled; and freedom from bondage to alcohol, drug and sexual addictions is renewing lives throughout the nations. God's overpowering love song for all his creation continues in steady melodies of care and hope. Truthfully, there are more Christians in Asia, Indonesia, Africa, The Middle East and Russia than there are in all the Western nations combined.

No one, especially, this unassuming Dutchman, envisioned a worldwide organization successfully smuggling millions of Bibles into Iron Curtain countries, China, The Middle East, and Africa when their governments forbid all things Christian. Nor did he conceive that under the leadership of the Holy Spirit, Open Doors could lovingly impact Muslims, Palestinians, their Jewish brothers and sisters in the Middle East and peoples of all religions worldwide.

"Lord, thank you that even though we are in the midst of a spiritual battle, the victory is already yours. Help us to proclaim that victory today, Amen."

Brother Andrew has passed the CEO leadership torch to James Curry, but he still communicates through the computer, newsletters, radio and TV the good news of the Gospel's Kingdom love.

Open Doors' Ministry definition:

1) To strengthen the body of Christ living under restriction or persecution by providing and delivering Bibles, and other helps, and encouraging it to become involved in world evangelism.

2) To train and encourage the body of Christ in threatened or unstable areas preparing believers to face persecution and suffering, and equip them to maintain a witness to the gospel of Christ.

3) To motivate, mobilize and educate the church in the free world to identify with and become more involved in assisting the suffering church, believing that when "one members suffers, all the members suffer with it.".

---

1) "For The Love of my Brothers" by Brother Andrew and Verne Becker

2) "Their Blood Cries Out" by Paul Marshall with Lela Gilbert
3) "Light Force" by Brother Andrew and Al Janssen

To contact Open Doors: Ex-officio Director, President and CEO, David Curry

P.O. box 27001, Santa Ana, CA 92799 USA

Phone 888-5-BIBLE-5 (888-524-2535) E-mail: opendoorsusa.org

GOD'S LOVE STORY
IN MY LANGAGE

he first translating of God's Word into people's native tongues came from the Holy Spirit on Pentecost, when diverse people of many nations heard the Apostles preaching. Each heard in their own language; thousands were baptized that day. Hearing God loves you in your own heart language confirms God knows and loves you. The early gospels, letters and epistles were written and distributed in Koine Greek, the trade language of the first century, and understood by rich and poor alike.

In our own time, Wycliffe Translators produce Bibles in all languages. Singles and couples are inspired to devote their lives to making God's Word available to each language and dialect around the world.

One of the modern-day translators, Mabel Giruard, was part of the wonderful youth group at Capitol Methodist Church, Phoenix, AZ during the 1940's. She attended college, married a nice man from Michigan, then they took off to Bolivia to translate the Bible into other dialects. Once in a while they came home to visit, and finally they retired with wonderful stories to tell. Mabel was a very devout Christian, the embodiment of sweetness. Thanks to Mabel and her family, there are many in Bolivia, Peru, and Brazil can read the Bible and know of God's love for them in their own native tongue.

The Wycliffe organization began when God led young Cameron Townsend to Guatemala in 1917 to sell Spanish Bibles. He was surprised that most of the people did not understand Spanish, but spoke their own beautiful Cakchiquel, a very complex language. He learned it and painstakingly over a 10-year period, created an alphabet, grammar and translated the New Testament into Cakchiquel.

Townsend opened Camp Wycliffe in Arkansas in the summer of 1934, to train other young people to accomplish in other nations what he had done in Guatemala. He chose the name Wycliffe, to honor John Wycliffe, the first person to translate the entire Bible, into English in 1382. Until then, the Latin Vulgate Bible was only available to Priests and teachers who read and taught its precepts to the congregations.

Townsend honored the man who influenced the religious world long before Martin Luther, with logic and controversial theology such as 'a person's knowledge of the Bible would guide him or her in grace.' A reformer and Oxford university teacher, John Wycliffe is considered the 'Morning Star' of the Reformation. He believed in three very controversial ideas: 1) One's personal life should be based on the Bible, not just by observing the Church Sacraments;

2) The holiness of a person is more important than their church title (Priest, Vicar, etc); and

3) He was appalled at the pomp and luxury of the church leaders.

A major philosopher, Wycliffe felt that all persons needed to and could utilize logic. One of his famous sayings was "We concern ourselves with the verities that are and leave aside the errors which arise for speculation on matters which are not." He died a natural death; however Hus and many reformers who followed him were burned at the stake for similar ideals.

John Wycliffe's wisdom and belief in people reading the Bible in their own language remains the goal of the worldwide Wycliffe Global Alliance (WGA) with 45 Member and more than 60 Partner Organizations. Multicultural and multinational, the WGA is flexible enough to serve under God's direction in an ever- changing world.

Two students enrolled at Townsend's first 1934 Arkansas meeting, which improved to five men in attendance the following year. He took the five to Mexico to begin field work. From this small beginning 81 years ago teams have grown across Africa, Asia, Australia, Europe, The Middle East, North and Central America. Two-thirds of the worlds' languages and dialects have all or part of the Bible. Yet, over 2,000 of the world's 6,900 languages do not have one verse of God's Word.

The 12-member Global Leadership Team gives guidance and direction, advises and consults with the international ministry networks and partnerships. Wycliffe bases its philosophy on Townsend's Protestantism which regards the intercultural and multilinguistic spread of Christianity as a divine command. They adhere to the principle of *sola scriptura* by regarding Biblical texts as the authoritative and infallible word of God.

In addition to the translators, many of whom are native to their country, there are team members who construct offices and homes, mechanics who maintain the trucks and equipment and pilots who ferry people in and out of jungles and remote villages. Some positions are paid, but many of the personnel raise financial support from churches, families and communities to pay their salaries. This is common to several of the great non-governmental entities supplying food, medical care, education, fresh water pumps, sewing machines, farm equipment, animals and seeds to help people earn a living and live a healthy lifestyle. This work is under the Wycliffe Association Group.

The Larsons are an example of what life is like for modern day families when they undertake a role for Wycliffe Associates. This young American couple and their two children are in Papua New Guinea where Evan Larson specializes in mechanics and welding. He had spent time in New Guinea before and speaks the language which comes easy to him. Home to seven million people, the terrain is rugged, causing breakdowns of vehicles frequently in the dry weather, as roads are impossible to navigate in the wet season.

Evan felt drawn to missionary work since high school and his wife, Elizabeth also. He keeps the equipment rolling and the generators working for the frequent showing of The Jesus Film in the native dialects. As one woman said, "Having the Bible in *English only* is like holding a cold glass of water that we cannot drink."

Evan and Elizabeth are located at the resource center in Ukarumpa where there is also a medical center, a print shop, auto shop, general store, construction and maintenance facilities. Along with his job of keeping the vehicles working, Evan trains locals in mechanics and welding. Surely they miss home. As one of the children has been sick Evan is back in USA upgrading welding.

When Westerners send our missionaries to the rest of the world they come with Western clothes, food and habits. However, the Bible contains not only spiritual, but God's basic format for healthy, happy people anywhere, in any location, speaking any language. When the words of God's love are in your own language, you know God is talking to you where you are just as you are.

One great scientific advance is the solar operating unit allowing Print on Demand and immediate communications between teams. It has speeded up translations by many months worldwide. There is a need for more of these units. There is also a new system called MAST which speeds up the methodology so that weeks instead of months and years can yield accurate translations. The WGA hopes to have scriptures for every language worldwide by 2020.

To acquaint people with the progress being made and Wycliffe's goals and needs, many cities hold annual dinners open to the public. Team members from the field share the exciting progress being made. It allows all to share and invest in Kingdom building. All Wycliffe field work is done in cooperation with the host governments, universities and philanthropic groups.

Wycliffe Associates has many heroes like the late Dr. John Bendor-Samuel of the UK. He took a course and became excited about the possibilities and pioneered the cause of Bible translation across Africa, where he spearheaded the drive for Ghana, Nigeria, Togo, Cameroon, Ivory Coast and Ethiopia. He served as UK Director, was speaker and lecturer around the world, and served as editor of Journal of West African Linguistics. Roger Welch said, "John's vision was to see the Bible translated into all vernacular languages, but above all, he was quite simply, one of the finest Christian men I have ever known."

If you wish to know what transformation occurs by having the Bible introduced to people in their native language in love, be sure to read the Acua Indians in the next chapter. One of its heroines, Elisabeth Elliot, passed away June 2015. You can read how an entire civilization changed from Stone Age people, living in rural

Ecuador to modern citizens. After five husband's deaths, the wives and families of those missionaries came to the Auca Indians writing and speaking their Auca language in Godly love. This was possible because of the translation of the Bible into their Auca language by Wycliffe Translators. Over eighty-five percent of the Aucas are Christians, who no longer kill all strangers with spears. Their young people attend college and run their nation. It is an amazing, real life story of Kingdom Love in action, thanks to having a Bible in their native language, along with caring Christian missionaries who loved and discipled them.

BASIC WYCLIFFE BELIEFS

Christianity is relationship. It's about who we believe in.
- We believe the Bible, the inspired Word of God, is completely trustworthy, speaking with supreme authority in all matters of belief and practice.
- We believe in one God, who exists eternally in three persons, the Father, The Son and the Holy Spirit.
- We believe all people being created in the image of God, have intrinsic value, but as a result of sin are alienated from God and each other, and therefore in need of reconciliation.
- We believe that Jesus Christ, the Son of God, born of the virgin Mary, is fully God and fully human; He demonstrated God's love for sinners by suffering the penalty of death in their place, rose bodily from the dead and ascended to heaven where He intercedes for His people.
- We believe all who repent and trust in Jesus Christ alone as Lord and Savior are, by the grace of God, declared to be right with Him, receiving forgiveness and eternal life.
- We believe the Lord Jesus Christ will return personally in glory, raise the dead and judge the world,
- We believe all people will rise from the dead, those who are in Christ to enjoy eternal life with God and those who are lost to suffer eternal separation from Him.
- We believe in the Holy Spirit who imparts new life to those who believe in Christ, through His indwelling presence and

transforming power He gives assurance and equips believers for holy living and effective service.
- We believe the Church is the body of Christ, the fellowship of all believers and is commissioned to make disciples of all nations.

*Material is from Wycliffe Associates Web Sites,
*Wikipedia,
* letters from Evan and Elizabeth Larson, and
*Memories of Mabel Giruard.

Contact Information: E-mail: wa_ prayer@wycliffeassociaites.org

1) Wycliffe Associates, Bruce Smith, President/CEO, 11450 Transition Way, (P. O. Box 620143), Orlando, Fl 32682 Phone 1-407-852-3800

2) Wycliffe Bible Translators, Bob Creson, President, 11221 John Wycliffe Blvd., Orlando, FL 32832 Phone 1-800-992-5433

3) SIL International–Dr. Frederick A.Boswell, Exec. Director 7500 W. Camp Wisdom Rd., Dallas, TX 75236-5629 USA Phone 1 972-708-7400

4) JAARS–Woody McLendon, President, P.O. Box 248, Waxhaw, NC 28173

5) Seed Company–Todd Peterson, President 3030 Matlock Rd., Suite 104, Arlington, TX 76015 Phone 817-557-2121

EVERY ACT OF LOVE COUNTS

*"Go, therefore and make disciples of all the nations,
baptizing them in the name of the Father, and of the
Son and of the Holy Spirit, teaching them to observe
all things that I have commanded you; and lo, I
am with you always, even to the end of the age."*
Matt: 28: 19-20 NKJV

*I*n 1955 our little Evangelical United Brethren Church heard from
a young couple who wanted to raise money for a mission trip
and challenge us to grant financial support. They had met a wonderful Auca lady named Dayuma from Ecuador. Dayuma converted
to Christ while living away from her tribe, and wanted her people to
know about God's love. This couple felt called by God to reach out
to the Aucas's.

Jim and Elisabeth Elliot were a nice couple and though I tossed
$10 into the plate and pledged support (at that time it was worth more
than it is now), I wondered why anyone would feel compelled to travel
to some remote Ecuadorian Indian village to reach the Huaorani tribe,
living like Stone Agers, commonly called The Aucas. They excitedly
told us they were one of five couples involved. The husbands would
fly in, visit the Aucas, and then the wives and children would follow.
The church pledged to support their mission. Thus our little church
became involved with the Acua Missionaries.

However, the Aucas had been frequently troubled by major oil
companies trampling all over their land as well chicle (gum) and

144

rubber hunters, who ravished their women and destroyed parts of their jungles. The Aucas found it necessary to hide when strangers were around, or kill them with spears, their only weapons.

The five men flew over the territory and dropped gifts of food and toys for the children, then one day landed where they had seen activity. Not knowing the Acua language and wearing western clothes, the Aucas viewed them as they viewed all strangers, as enemies. Some warriors came and spear-killed all five of them. On the surface it appears senseless and totally wrong to kill five men who came out of love with a desire to reach out in friendship. No people had appeared who cared about the Aucas, only men seeking products and wealth, who thought these natives and their families were sub-humans existing in a jungle, questioning whether the Aucas even owned the land. With only negative experiences from outsiders, why should the Aucas trust these five strange men in the airplane? When they landed neither group could understand the other. Unfortunately, disdainful intrusion by past wealth seekers, ignorance of the Aucas' language killed five innocent men.

Despite their husbands death at the hands of the Acuas and knowing only 500 Auca words , Rachel Saint, Elisabeth Elliot, and the three other widows with their children, along with Dayuma returned to the Auca area in Ecuador. These missionaries lived among the Aucas demonstrating the good news of Christ's love and forgiveness in the Auca language. These brave women and children presented no threat to the Aucas who came to the saving knowledge of Jesus Christ. The men who had killed the five husbands were baptized. In fact, the man who killed Jim Elliott baptized one of Jim's sons later in the Ara Huno River where the five men were speared. Another, who had killed Steve Saint's father, gave his spear to Steve so that Steve could kill him. Instead they became good friends.

Skip ahead. In 2012 I was attending a small Bible study in our retirement community along with an elderly man, Mac McCourry a regular attender. He usually sat quietly, commenting rarely. When he spoke it was with love and reverence about God's Word and His forgiveness to Mac. Through the weeks he made sage remarks with deep humility. Little snippets would come out indicating he had done some translating. So I asked him point blank what he had done in the past as he mentioned Wycliffe Translators. "Oh I translated for some Indians," he replied. "Western, or Eastern Indians?" I continued. "Western...some from Ecuador," he answered.

Something clicked in my thinking...was it the Auca's? And yes, he had translated 500 words of the Auca Indian language and a Auca New Testament to prepare Rachel Saint, Elisabeth, and the others so that they could speak Auca and teach from the Acua Bible when they returned to Ecuador. When I asked if he knew Elisabeth Elliot, he smiled broadly and said, "Yes, I knew Rachel, who died from cancer and is buried in Acua territory, Betty, and the others. In fact, my wife and I lived for a year with the Aucas."

He was humble, not thinking his part was particularly important. But his translation was the instrument that permitted the returning missionaries to share the Gospel in the Auca language. It touched these native people who have been around longer than North Americans, to hear God's great love story in words they understood; to meet outsiders who were neither harming their families nor trying to take their property.

Currently the Aucas have been impacted by the discovery of vast oil reserves on their lands. They ably negotiated arrangements, retaining a large portion of their lands for living while allocating areas for industrial development. Their young men and women attend college, if they wish. Their lives are a far cry from those spear- wielding hunters who killed five young missionaries in 1955. (A friend's grand daughter's dated one of the Auca young men in college).

Elisabeth Elliot's wonderful book *Through Gates of Splendor,* a best seller, was made into a documentary in 1957. The movie "End of the Spear" shot on location in Ecuador, features some of the Aucas playing themselves as they tell how Kingdom Love was brought to them, enriching their lives forever.

When Christians are motivated by Kingdom Love they never know what doors might open for taking God's word to the world. This humble man, Mac McCourry, spent time translating an obscure language. His work enabled the missionaries to reach a whole tribe of people who a few years earlier killed outsiders in order to survive, but are now safe, secure christians.

My heart warmed when I realized that my little church along with people like Mac played a part in Kingdom building by our contributions and prayers. If only we could see to connect the dots in the wonders of God's world, the little ones as well as the big ones, we would see how He is able to utilize our little contributions here and there, combining the right ingredients for wonderful miracles.

When we get to heaven and gain more understanding, we will be surprised at seemingly unimportant spiritual acts bringing salvation to people's lives, Holy Spirit led actions large and small, several years and miles apart, mysteriously combine to reconcile men and God. We serve an awesome God!

Mac McCourry has given permission for the article to be printed.

For a deeper look at this modern miracle: Read *"Through Gates of Splendor"* by Elisabeth Elliot and view a copy of the movie ""End of the Spear." which actually features some of the Acuas and their faith stories.

Good Samaritans-Medical Teams International

"A certain man went down from Jerusalem to Jericho and fell among thieves who stripped him of his clothing, wounded him... But a certain Samaritan ... had compassion..."   Luke 10:30,33 NKJV

The Good Samaritan left money with the owner of the Inn for room and food for the wounded man he found on the road. He also promised to pay more if it was due when he returned. Most are conscious the moment when we do a good deed, but not where that action might lead us. However, as one learns, God sees now and ahead into future needs as well.

Sitting comfortably in his Salem, Oregon living room watching the news with his wife Jean, in 1979, Ron Post was struck with the awful plight of 40,000 refugees from the "Killing Fields" of Pol Pot in Cambodia. They escapees fled to Thailand to a seven acre area where they were crammed together with no refinements. Ron Post felt a deep concern and then God spoke to him to gather up a team of doctors in two weeks and go help those people. Ron argued with himself about this request, but it fell into place piece by piece. A Christian businessman, unacquainted with such situations he was at a loss, but followed the spiritual prompting which led him to caring associates, politicians, doctors, nurses, supplies, and finally Eastern

Airlines who would fly the team and equipment to Thailand...within the two week criteria.

Ron and Jean and their basic group found they were seeking purpose in life and had come face to face with intense hunger, sickness, pain, work and burdens, and as well as face to face with Jesus who would look at them through the eyes of the 'least of these.'

The refugee area smelled from open trenches filled with human waste and the shrunken people who were receiving three tablespoons of rice per day. This team from the northwest worked with World Vision International setting up a 125 bed ward to help heal the sick.

"What terrible sufferings! The stench, the wailing, groaning and emaciated bodies fighting disease... I felt out of place, confused and insufficient, I felt exactly the way God wanted me to feel," Ron realized.

Upon the tour's completion and recuperation from a mild illness the idea of Northwest Medical Teams (now MTI) as a permanent organization, formed in his mind as if Ron had been planning the mission for years. Medical Teams International was created by God through Ron and his associates, to demonstrate the love of Christ to those in crisis. Ron, upon sound advice, set up a basic team who in turn set up long range plans, accountability with annual audits, and membership in BBB and ECFA.*

"Like strands of rope woven together, people from all backgrounds joined to make this mission work," said Ron Post of the very first mission to Thailand and hundreds since then.

Thus in 1979 was born one of the most active, vital medical service groups in the world. They came to aid Mexico City after the earthquake in 1986 and since have on-going facilities for the ' trashpickers' living in the huge dumps. The lives of thousands who live in the dumps, eating tossed out garbage, having no latrines, showers, or homes, have been dramatically improved. God led MTI teams to build showers, latrines, classrooms, medical clinics on the spot and elsewhere in Mexico City, demonstrating the love of Christ to those in need. The first Bible Club in the dumps began with a few and now 3,000 attend weekly. Multitudes of those poverty born people have learned to read, to sew, work and actually are able to leave the trash picking life behind. One of the graduating students spoke regarding what school meant to her." Here I learned a skill that will greatly benefit my family. And here, I have gained self-worth."

Mexico City, like Cairo and many other major cities are home to millions surviving in the dumps and living out of makeshift cardboard houses. Often more people actually live in the dumps than in the cities themselves.

The Ethiopian famine due to drought challenged MTI teams greatly as they flew in and were sent to a number of intensive feeding and care units. The nurses worked at trying to feed severely dehydrated babies with the special formula. For some it worked while other babies were too near death to even take in the nourishment. One nurse had tears in her eyes as she laid down a baby and said "We lost the baby. Every night, I go back to my tent and get on my knees asking God to forgive me for not saving more."

Ron Post's heart ached for the team members as they saved hundreds, yet mourned every person that was lost. One nurse, Diane Vann Order told a reporter who asked, "What do you think you can accomplish among all these sick and dying people?" She thought for a moment and said, "Well, I guess we are giving them today. Maybe they will have tomorrow." Inspired MTI members felt a fresh determination sweeping over their hearts, to help as many people as they could.

In 1988 the Flying Tigers Airline flew help to the Armenians after their earthquake which left well over 120,000 dead. And so it has continued each year as hurricanes, tsunamis, earthquakes, wars, disease, and droughts impact various parts of the world.

On the 1990 evening news, disfigured Romanian orphans called 'Irrecoverable' in the orphanages shocked the western world. After some negotiations, Evergreen Airlines flew MIT teams into Romania to help with the "irrecoverable" children...those with blemishes, who were ware-housed like caged animals. Some were rarely touched, barely surviving on limited food and often were cold. Broken windows and plumbing were never repaired. No one was permitted to adopt these children until MTI came in to operate, changing the cleft palates, crooked feet and crossed eyes. Afterwards, many were adopted into loving homes in the west.

The original MTI doctors share their stories which encourage new doctors and nurses to work the next trip, trained by the experienced doctors. Trips into earthquakes, wars, starvation or disease are never easy to face as medical teams do everything possible to salvage people harmed by disasters. Some can be helped; some cannot. Many nights, tired and faced with emotional stress, team members fall exhausted on their cots with tears and lots of prayers.

MTI flew into Northern Iraq to aid the Kurds, the largest group of people in the world with no country, some 22 million in 1988. Saddam Hussein had killed many. The MTI teams, not only helped the Kurdish people, but also obtained vaccines for their cattle, helping the animals survive to work and be available for food. The Western Christian groups were the only ones helping the Kurds.

MTI has grown to an annual outlay of $136 million in equipment, medicine, food and seeds going to aid others. Donations from medical equipment and pharmaceutical companies are fostered so that 97% of any donations go directly to help the people in need, not overhead. Teams grow as the disasters continue. The Tigard, Oregon plant has over 200 volunteers each week packing medicines, equipment, tools and supplies for shipment to other nations as well as for the medical teams themselves. Often, MTI works with the Red Cross, World Vision and other non-government organizations (NGO's), supplying the medical backup for relief efforts.

Current President and CEO of MTI, Jeff Pinneo brought experience from his leadership at Horizon and Alaska Airlines in 2012, becoming the third leader. Under Jeff's leadership the ambitious plan for MTI is to double the work among people around the world who are affected by disaster, conflict and poverty by 2020. Like Ron Post before him, Jeff is surrounded by very capable, visionary, compassionate team members, all with humanitarian experience in finance, emergency relief, health, human services and fundraising.

Life is never the same for doctor, dentists, nurses, technical supporters and volunteers, once they have been to Rwanda, Uganda, Mexico, Guatemala, Myanmar, Haiti, Japan, northern and western Africa. Saving hundreds of lives moves team members to make trips again and again.

One such person is Dr. Randall Jacobs, Bend, Oregon who served with MTI in Uganda, Kenya and Somalia. Dr. Randy explained when asked about close calls, "It is not quiet and peaceful. Armed escorts were required in Eastern Kenya and Western Somalia due to Al Shabab activity and banditry/kidnappers. While we were there other NGO's including Samaritan's Purse were shot at and pursued by kidnappers, but thankfully no one was seriously injured and they escaped. It's part of the daily landscape in that area." Asked about some memorable events he recalled. "God's protection for our team while in Somalia – as we were treating displaced persons due to famine in Dhobley. Shabab and Kenya military were within ear shot. On another trip, working in a UN refugee camp in southwest Uganda (Nakavali) we were treating 24,000 newly arrived Congolese refugees from western Congo. God's provision was amazing, providing enough materials and the energy for the staff to treat 300 patients daily suffering from severe malaria, pneumonia and dysentery. We treated over 4,000 in a month, no deaths."

When asked how his life changed by working with MTI there was a surprise answer. Dr. Randy continued, "After returning from my first trip to northern Uganda working in camps for displaced persons following the Lord's Resistance Army incursion in that area, I was compelled to look for needs in Central Oregon. God pointed me to the Shepherd's House – A Christian mission and residential program for men. I began a weekly free clinic there and over the years was part of developing a volunteer mobile medical program to the homeless in our community. This program has now been incorporated into Mosaic Medical – a Federally Qualified Health Center (FQHC*) in central Oregon with multiple fixed clinics in three counties."

Dr. Randy concluded with thoughts about the MTI. "So many refugees need care in Syria, Iraq, Afghanistan, Somalia, but it is just too dangerous for westerners. Staffing by native professionals works well. US volunteers work alongside providing care and teaching. I am a member of the Disaster Response Team. We must continue praying for God's intervention and peace in those regions. God makes a way, the response to Ebola is a good example. Churches and mission groups partner better. Pray first of all."

The calling to reach out further is typical of those who answer the MTI call. Many of the doctors and dentists, like Dr. Randy, have reached out into their communities to those in need. MTI itself has four mobile dental clinics operating here in Oregon for the poor. Medicaid provides medical help, but does not provide dental care. MTI helps fill that gap.

MTI has jobs for all skills from actual packing, calling or traveling to locations, to praying daily for the teams and the people being touched and healed. My former missionary friends, pack medical supplies two days a week at MTI–and pray a lot for the teams.

Rich in fulfillment of saving thousands of lives, love and knowledge of doing God's work among the most helpless people, MTI teams continue to demonstrate the love of Christ to those in crisis, who in turn learn God loves them and they are worth while persons. The MTI Motto is: 'Accountable to God and man,' truly fitting for MTI associates, these modern day Good Samaritans.

---

* Jeff Pinneo, President and CEO of MTI
- BBB Better Business Bureau
- ECFA Evangelical Council For Financial Accountability
- **"Created For A Purpose"** by Ron Post Ron's account of the MTI story is recommended reading for everyone. You will see the living reality for the world's truly poor and the 'eyes of your heart' will be opened. The quotations from this article come from Ron Post's book, unless noted otherwise.
- Dr. Randall Jacobs, Bend Oregon. It seemed appropriate to look at MTI through the eyes of a doctor who has been there and served.
- www.mosaicmedical.org – a Federally Qualified Health Center and non-profit
- Diane Vann Order, Nurse for MTI Team.

Contact Information: Medical Teams International: P. O. Box 10, Portland, Oregon 97207, Phone: 503-624-1000

KINGDOM LOVE
ENDURES FOREVER

You shall not take vengeance, nor bear any grudge
against the children of your people, but you shall
love your neighbor as yourself: I AM the LORD."
                                        Lev. 19:18 NKJV

Can anyone document when Kingdom Love arrived on earth?
Did it arrive with Jesus when he came to share God face to face
with the people? Jesus mentioned the Kingdom is near you, which
some took to mean He was representing the future eternal Kingdom.
    Kingdom Love has been with mankind from the beginning.
Perhaps one early example was God making clothes from animal
skins to cover Adam and Eve's nakedness. It came to the old couple,
Abraham and Sarah, long past the child bearing years, with birth of
son Isaac. It saved Ishmael and Hagar with water in the desert. Both
the Old and New Testaments are filled with examples. The prophet
Isaiah gave hope to the exiles in Babylon when he prophesied 100
years before Cyrus' decree, 'the captured Jews would depart from
Babylon to rebuild their own land.' Kingdom Love enabled Esther to
save her people from genocide. Through prophets people were raised
from the dead. The ravens fed Elijah as he ran from Jezebel; and wet
and dry fleece guided Gideon. Jesus met with sinners like prostitutes,
publicans, tax collectors, forgave them and healed them. Willingly
He died on the cross to reconcile all of us sinners to God, the source

of light, truth, healing and comfort for every person from societies' least to prestigious officials. And yes, just as early Christians were jailed and killed for faith in Jesus, so in many lands today, the cost of discipleship comes at a great personal sacrifice, imprisonment and even death. However, believers know it is worth the price.

Kingdom Love connections are at work 24/7. For example, a Sunday school teacher visited one of his students who was a little rough around the edges, at his shoe store workplace. He wanted to let him know he was appreciative of the how hard the boy worked and still made the effort to attend church on Sundays. He spoke with him about salvation, leading him to faith in the Lord with friendship and tears. That young student was none other than the powerful evangelist, Dwight L. Moody, who turned America and The United Kingdom upside down in the late 1870's-1900. His huge ministry included Pastors F. B. Meyer and J. W. Chapman, and a professional baseball player, named Billy Sunday.

Billy Sunday started an outreach to baseball players and other young men. One of his fellow evangelists in the 1920's was Mordecai Ham who was asked to preach in North Carolina where people had been praying for help with their churches and young people. One night when Ham preached a teenager named Billy Graham came forward, 'deciding to give his life to Christ.' Billy Graham and a young Bob Pierce were active together in a movement called Youth for Christ until China stole Bob's heart and he founded World Vision. Billy became the World's Evangelist for several decades. A long line of Kingdom Love impacted millions around the world because of a praying Sunday school teacher.

Kingdom Love preachers, brothers Charles and John Wesley, were born into a home having a great teaching mother and spiritual father. At this period of history thousands of Brits had no jobs or hope. The Wesley's' openly shared God's love through exhortation and Bible Study as well as giving personal help and comfort to suffering people. They spent their lives making disciples, who in turn educated more disciples, making such a difference, that many credit their caring gospel preaching with keeping England from collapsing into a bloody revolution like France suffered.

Later, some of Wesley's disciples mentored young William Booth who founded The Salvation Army (TSA) in 1864. For 150 years, in many nations, TSA still brings salvation and help to people in 126 nations. TSA feeds the hungry, helps addicts leave that destructive lifestyle replacing it with Kingdom Love–much more fulfilling than alcohol and/or drugs. Those little red kettles, those bands of lads and lassies still tell the old story: God loves you and so do I.

Brother Andrew enjoyed his nights of putting sugar into gas tanks of occupying Nazi soldiers, before he instigated Kingdom Love through food, blankets, and Bibles in all languages, especially in nations who outlaw them. Andrew recognized people's physical needs, and great hunger for God's word. From one little Volkswagen Beetle filled with Bibles, his work grew worldwide into nations where Christians say, "It is not a matter of "If I will be killed or imprisoned, but when." However they continue to extend Kingdom Love to all whom they can reach, willing to pay the same price that all Jesus' original Disciples paid, refusing to recant their love and faith in Jesus Christ.

Life's struggles have always been about who is in charge of the nations, men? Or God? As Theologian R.C. Sproul stated, " Even most Christians salute the sovereignty of God, but believe in the sovereignty of man."

Kings and world armies have been coming and going since time began. Schools teach the rise of Egyptians, Babylonians, Hebrews, Medes and Persians, Greeks and then the Roman Empire. There were the Chinese who invented gun powder, china dishes, writing and also the hordes under Genghis Khan who came across Asia, stealing the food supplies and taking slaves. The Syrians, Persians and their heirs ruled the Mediterranean and North African areas for hundreds of years, while Europe and the Christian Church also held sway in the Western world. Amidst endless wars thousands of Christians lived peacefully for centuries in the Middle East side by side with Arabs and Jews.

Colonization of Africa for its natural resources occurred across the ages. While in early 1800's missionaries brought Kingdom Love to the varied African tribes and nations, Muhammad ibn Abd al Wahhab founded strict Sharia Law in Egypt and Saudi Arabia.

Businessmen brought both good and harm to the native people by extraction of minerals jewels and gold. Conquering tribes made slaves of their captives, selling them to each other as well as Westerners and Middle East nations. In fact, slave trade still exists in parts of Africa and the Middle East. By contrast at the same time millions of lives were improved by Kingdom Love taught by David Livingston, Albert Schweitzer and hundreds of pastors, nuns, priests, missionaries, teachers and medical personnel.

Christians, Jews and many religious other groups know love is stronger than hate. Kingdom Love must multiply exponentially so that the world will experience the love and peace that God desires for every person, rather than be forced into a sixth century Caliphate by ISIS or a Middle Eastern nuclear war.

Today the world stands at the dangerous crossroads; do we want life? or destruction?

Humankind when reconciled to God receives His love, forgiveness, grace and blessings. Blessings flow to our neighbors – then to their neighbors. Kingdom love ceaselessly impacts lives when each puts the Great Commandment into practice. What do you suppose is in store for you the next time you practice loving God with all your heart and your neighbor as yourself?

ACKNOWLEDGEMENTS

*A*t the 2009 Oregon Christian Writers Summer Conference, the Holy Spirit spoke to me in audible words, "Why don't you write about the heroes of the faith?"

It is astounding how one person's special action can start events felt sooner or later around the world, in God's never-ceasing efforts to reconcile mankind. Checks from unknown sources show up at the very last minute when the food is gone. People from all walks of life are impacted by programs implemented by compassionate persons thousands of miles away. First, I thank God for His countless blessings.

I wish to thank my daughter Wendy Bryant for reading chapters well as rest of family, Cindy and Brian, Christy, Gil and Carmen, and Michael, and Sean Waple's art. A very special bravo for childhood friend, B. J. Livermore who stands beside this book's values. Thank you is due to my Oregon Christian Writers Critique Group: Gordon Grose, Shirley Dechaine, Paul Hailey, Stan Torrance, Bob Nipper, Lillian Penner and the late Marlene Yount, who patiently listened to this entire book, some chapters more than once, giving valuable input.

These are but a few of real life examples of God's love in measureable, genuine actions when ordinary people say 'yes' to the Holy Spirit.

Dwight L. Moody's Sunday School Teacher, who schooled many disciples, was just being a caring teacher. Jim and Elisabeth Elliot, Rachel Saint and the others felt called to bring Jesus' story to the

Auca Indians. India Pastor K.P. Yohannan continues to be strongly motivated by the deep needs of Asians to hear the Gospel, as were Rev. Harry Haines and Bob Pierce; The Asian and African converts to Christianity are blessed with frequent signs and wonders. Bro Andrew never waivered from the time he felt called to reach out to Christians whose faith had been outlawed, just as the late Herbert Hoover's great heart and service to many people was rarely known. Quietly he kept blessings in motion, saving millions from starvation while improving life for common men and women, especially the youth.

I am grateful to many people at each of these splendid organizations:

*   Dr. John Haines; Son of the late Harry Haines, **Former UMCOR Director**
*   Major Barbara Blix, **The SalvationArmy**;
*   **Syracuse University and Norman Gersham** for permission to use **"Besa"** materials;
*   **World Vision:** Rich Stearns, Pres./ CEO; Steve Reynolds, Director of Advocacy, Integration and Campaigns; Jane Sutton-Redner, Editorial Director, Content, Curation, Mobilization; Marilee Pierce Dunker, Child Advocate/ Advocacy and Communications Director, and Laura Reed-Photo Librarian
*   Franklin Graham, **Samaritan's Purse;**
*   "Gandhi, an Interpretation" by **E. Stanley Jones**
*   K. P. Yohannan, Pres. / CEO, **Gospel for Asia;**
*   Jim Curry, US Pres/ CEO, **Open Doors,** Al Janssen and of course, **Brother Andrew**
*   Mac McCourry Elisabeth Elliot and the other Auca missionary Families, **The Auca Salvation Story,**
*   Donn Hallman, Bruce Smith, **Wycliffe Translators and Wycliffe Associates;**
*   Jeff Pinneo, Pres./ CEO **Medical Teams International;** Dr. Randall Jacobs and Angie Allee,
*   Matthew Schaefer and Lynn Smith, **Herbert Hoover Presidential Library-Museum,** Sarah Munro, the Hoover-Minthorn House

*   NKJV was source of all scriptures unless noted otherwise.

Billie felt led to write this particular book about the daily manifestations of God's love, often taken for granted. Kingdom Love gives a glimpse of the scope of activities by the God of the universe who loves mankind. Heroic spiritual works bring God's truth and grace across the globe to the least of the least as well as the best of the best, long after crisis headlines are gone."

CPSIA information can be obtained
at www.ICGtesting.com
Printed in the USA
FSOW02n0305281215
14844FS

9 781498 455756